The Spirituality of Anne Dutton
Selected Letters

The Spirituality of Anne Dutton

Edited by Priscilla Wong

The Spirituality of Anne Dutton: Selected Letters

Copyright © 2025 Priscilla Wong. All rights reserved. This book may not be reproduced, in whole or in part, without written permission from the publishers.

The Anne Dutton Project, Volume 1

H&E Academic, West Lorne, Ontario
www.hesedandemet.com

978-1-77484-175-4 (paperback)
978-1-77484-173-0 (hardback)
978-1-77484-174-7 (eBook)

In memory of my dear friend Susan

Contents

The Anne Dutton Project	ix
Introduction	1

PART I Walking with God

Provenance	35
1. A Discourse upon Walking with God	39

PART II Letters on Spiritual Subjects and Diverse Occasions

Provenance	73
2. Death and the Joys of Heaven	75
3. Discouragement in Pastoral Ministry	77
4. Walking by Faith Amidst Trial	83
5. God's Providence in Prosperity and Adversity	87
6. Fearing One's Spiritual State	89
7. Doubting One's Own Interest in Christ	93
8. Guilt Over One's Sins and Coming unto Christ with Freedom	97
9. Strengthening against Error	101
10. Discouragement in Gospel Ministry	105
11. Joy Amidst Hardship	107

PART III The General Duty of Love

Provenance	111
12. A Letter to All the Saints on the General Duty of Love	115

Acknowledgements	135
About the Author	137

Works Cited	139
Textual Notes and Emendations	141
Scripture Index	145

SERIES PREFACE
The Anne Dutton Project

The name of Anne Dutton (1692-1765) is not a household name among modern-day Baptists. But it should be, as we hope to demonstrate through the volumes being published in this series. My first encounter with the name was through some comments by the early twentieth-century British Baptist historian W. T. Whitley. In his words, she had a "censorious spirit" that was critical of both George Whitefield (1714-1770) and John Wesley (1703-1791), and indeed of the eighteenth-century evangelical revival in general:

> She took up the role of Sanballat rather than of Nehemiah. In an age when others were up and doing, she saw nothing better than to single out points of difference and put stumbling-blocks in the way. ... Her case is extreme, but her spirit was widely disseminated and this may account largely for the failure of the Particular Baptists to resume their role of evangelizing.[1]

She was indeed critical of Wesley's Arminian theology and his perfectionism. They exchanged correspondence between 1739 and 1743 before Wesley terminated their epistolary relationship after Dutton's *A Letter To the Reverend Mr. John Wesley. In Vindication of the Doctrines of Absolute, unconditional Election, Particular Redemption, Special Vocation, and Final Perseverance* (1743). But Whitley failed to mention that Whitefield was also critical of his friend regarding the very same doctrinal issues.

---

[1] W. T. Whitley, *A History of British Baptists* (London: Charles Griffin & Co., 1923), 214-215.

The Spirituality of Anne Dutton

Whitefield viewed Dutton quite positively. He visited her on more than one occasion and promoted her books in America.[2] One of his early co-workers, William Seward (1702-1740), also corresponded with Dutton, and regarded her as a "choice servant of Christ."[3] In a letter that Seward received from her in May of 1739, he commented that it was "full of such comforts and direct answers from what I had been writing, that it filled my eyes with tears of joy. O how sweet is the balm of Gilead to a wounded soul."[4] Writing to her the following year, he again shared with her his "doubts and fears," especially with regard to the reality of his faith. He hoped "to receive comfort from her precious answers."[5] And when the Baptist cause in Cambridge was seeking a new pastor in the late 1750s, she heartily recommended one of Whitefield's converts, namely, Robert Robinson (1735-1790), who was a zealous Evangelical at the time.

While there is little doubt that she was a woman "of strong will and conviction,"[6] it is also clear that she played a critical role in the evangelical revivals of her day as a spiritual counselor and the author of a significant body of literature. Our hope is that the volumes in this small series will aid in the recovery of her rightful place in the world of eighteenth-century Evangelicalism.[7]

Michael A.G. Azad Haykin
Series editor

---

[2] Stephen J. Stein, "A Note on Anne Dutton, Eighteenth-Century Evangelical," *Church History* 44 (1975): 485-491.

[3] William Seward, *Journal of a Voyage from Savannah to Philadelphia, and from Philadelphia to England, M,DCC.XL* (London, 1740), 57.

[4] Seward, *Journal*, 57.

[5] Seward, *Journal*, 57.

[6] Stein, "A Note on Anne Dutton," 490.

[7] It should be noted that here is a seven-volume set of her works edited by JoAnn Ford Watson, *Selected Spiritual Writings of Anne Dutton: Eighteenth-Century, British-Baptist, Woman Theologian* (Macon, GA: Mercer University Press 2003-2015).

Introduction

The corpus of spiritual writings left to us by Anne Dutton (1692–1765), hymns, poems, epistles, essays, tracts, and memoir—while impressive—is only secondary to the spirit in which they were written. A memorial stone erected in 1887 preserves the literary legacy of this British Calvinist Baptist: 25 volumes of letters and 38 other works. Dutton's spiritual journey, chronicled in her three-part autobiography, published in her fifties, had ultimately led her to form the conviction that her skill with the pen was to be a dedicated means of ministering to souls: "This, through grace, I can say in general, that I have purely aimed at the glory of God and the good of souls in all the little pieces I have written and published."[1] Nearly a year before her death when she was 72 years old, suffering from throat ulcers, barely able to speak or swallow, she nonetheless persevered in the duty, writing feverishly to her numerous correspondents both at and around home and in America. One witness reported that she would write for sixteen to eighteen hours a day and bemoan the time that she had lost to eating, drinking, and sleeping.[2] In one letter, Dutton, while ill, advises a dear brother in Christ of the pressing need to redeem the time:

---

[1] JoAnn Ford Watson, *Selected Spiritual Writing of Anne Dutton, Eighteenth-Century British-Baptist, Woman Theologian: Volume 3: Autobiography* (Macon, GA: Mercer University, 2006), 161.

[2] John Andrews Jones in his Editor's Preface to Anne Dutton's *A Narration of the Wonders of Grace in Six Parts,* qtd. in JoAnn Ford Watson, *Selected Spiritual Writings of Anne Dutton: Eighteenth-century, British-Baptist, Theologian: Volume 2: Discourses, Poetry, Hymns, Memoir* (Macon, GA: Mercer University, 2004), 95.

The Spirituality of Anne Dutton

> I adore his grace that he let me do any thing for him so long. And I hope he will again let me do a little for him before he takes me home to the eternal enjoyment of himself. O my dear brother, prize and improve your time while health and strength last to serve in love the Lord your glorious lover. You will mourn when your time comes to an end that you have spent no more of it for the glory of Christ upon the earth.[3]

These historical glimpses intimate how Dutton became one of the most prolific female writers on theological subjects in the eighteenth-century. Most of her works, however, were published anonymously, often under the abbreviations "A.D."[4] This was to maximize the reception of her publications[5]: a woman publishing material on spiritual subjects was not a popular undertaking. The lack of rightful attribution is likely why much of her work had received marginal attention for such a long time.[6]

Over a century after her death, Baptist minister James Knight, editing a Dutton collection, keen on preventing her works from dipping into obscurity, paid great veneration in his preface to both her literary talents and deeply sanctified life:

> I value these works more than fine gold; they are jewels of the first water. Many times my soul has been completely ravished and caught heavenward—such is the life and power attending the reading thereof ... Both the style and matter of these letters

---

[3] Anne Dutton, *Letters on Spiritual Subjects, and Divers Occasions; Sent to Relations and Friends* (London: J. Hart, 1747), 89, Letter XXIV, To. Mr. W-----s, addressed as "My very dear brother."

[4] See Michael D. Sciretti Jr., "'Feed My Lambs': The Spiritual Direction Ministry of Calvinistic British Baptist Anne Dutton During the Early Years of Evangelical Revival" (Ph.D. diss., Baylor University, 2009), 175, for a discussion of Anne Dutton's signatures on her works.

[5] Stephen J. Stein, "A Note on Anne Dutton, Eighteenth-Century Evangelical," Church History, vol. 44, no. 4, [American Society of Church History, Cambridge University Press], 1975, see pp. 485, 487, 491. https://doi.org/10.2307/3163827.

[6] Consider Stein's remark: "Anonymity, forced or voluntary, has frequently cloaked the contributions of women to the life and thought of religious movements. Such was the case with Anne Dutton (1692–1765), an English evangelical, a 'gentlewoman' who appears fleetingly in the records of the eighteenth century and only momentarily in later annals of pious women." See "A Note on Anne Dutton," 485.

Introduction

declare the Authoress to have been an extraordinary woman, eminently taught of the Spirit, and possessing a depth of knowledge of the mysteries of the Kingdom of God far beyond what His children are generally favored with.[7]

Knight closed with his earnest hope for a future of like readers: "I now send this volume forth as bread cast upon the waters, hoping and praying that it may be found and eaten by many in days to come, when time with me shall be no more."

Floating silently on ocean waters are Dutton's writings—carried away on the ebb of time and only returning to shore when the winds have changed. Publisher George Keith printed a collection of Dutton's letters just years after her death, testifying that "Perhaps, very few, if any, of the Children of God, or Servants of the Lord in our Days, are favoured to walk so close with God as she did, or to have such frequent Communion with God in Christ, as she had."[8] In 1823–1824, collaborating with a pastor and a woman who had known Dutton personally, editor Christopher Goulding published a collection of Dutton's letters so that she would "no longer remain a stranger to the church of Christ; but her memory be rescued from oblivion…"[9] Around the same period, the second volume of *Memoirs of Eminently Pious Women* was published, which included a chapter on Dutton, the editor Samuel Burder introducing Dutton as "a woman of considerable abilities" and "great religious attainments."[10] Baptist pastor John Andrews Jones in 1833 assembled a collection of Dutton's works and implored its recipients to

> *read*, and the blessing of the Lord accompany the reading to thy soul … The author of the *lines* contained in this book, was a great

---

[7] Editor James Knight's "Compiler's Preface" qtd. in Watson, *Selected Spiritual Writings of Anne Dutton, Eighteenth-century British-Baptist, Woman Theologian: Volume 1, Letters* (Macon, GA: Mercer University, 2003), xxxvi.

[8] Sciretti, "Feed My Lambs," 8–9.

[9] *Letters on Spiritual Subjects* 1:V, qtd. in JoAnn Ford Watson, *Selected Spiritual Writings of Anne Dutton Eighteenth-century British-Baptist, Woman Theologian: Volume 6, Various Works* (Macon, GA: Mercer University, 2010), ix.

[10] Samuel Burder, *Memoirs of Eminently Pious Women, Volume 2* (London: J. Duncan, Longman, 1827), 227. This is Thomas Gibbon's first volume enlarged and revised.

saint. Her renewed mind was largely led into truth. The great and glorious doctrines of the everlasting gospel, she delighted in beyond expression. She had a deep insight into the native depravity of her heart; and, her experience of the grace of God upon her soul, with the *soul-liberty* granted her, was so blessed, that the plenitude thereof, as *she* experienced it, very rarely falls to the lot of the Lord's family, at least not in these days of "small things." – Zech. 4:10[11]

In 1884 Knight reprinted 103 of Dutton's letters.[12] Not until the next, next century would the winds stir the waters again. This once greatly lauded theologian and writer regained attention through the efforts of Dr. Michael A.G. Haykin, who fondly recalls riding a train while reading Dutton's letters (which had been gifted to him), and "despite the press of the commuters that morning," was "gripped by the spirituality of her prose."[13] Valuable has also been the conscientious work of JoAnn Ford Watson who released six volumes of Dutton's transcribed spiritual writings between the years of 2003 and 2010, granting greater accessibility to the general public to her works. And then, of course, there is the present series on Dutton that gives a comprehensive and in-depth look at her life, spirituality, and theology.

Sources of Dutton's spirituality
The sight of sparkling waves rolling toward us and what they have cast upon the shore ought to invite us oceanward; brushing the sand off this centuries-old treasure, we ought to ponder its origins that we might also feel in our hands the weightiness of the discovery.

---

[11] John Andrews Jones, in preface of Anne Dutton's *A Narration of the Wonders of Grace, In Six Parts* (London: W.M. Knight and Co., 1833), 2.
[12] Sciretti, "Feed My Lambs," 348.
[13] Michael A.G. Haykin, "A Cloud of Witnesses" (Evangelical Times, 2001). https://www.evangelical-times.org/articles/historical/a-cloud-of-witnesses-21/. Dr. Haykin had been gifted with *Selections from Letters on Spiritual Subjects*, compiled and published in 1884 by Mr Nigel Pibworth of Biggleswade. See his book *Eight Women of Faith* for a biographical sketch of Dutton's life.

Introduction

Consider the literature and figures from church history who influenced Dutton. Upon her death, she imparted all 212[14] of her books to Great Gransden, the Baptist church where her husband Benjamin Dutton had pastored from 1732 until his death in 1747. Future ministers could leaf through literature that she had held so dear, works by such greats as Martin Luther, John Calvin, and Jonathan Edwards, and those by seventeenth-century Puritans, including John Owen, Thomas Goodwin, and John Bunyan. The Puritans were foundational to Dutton's spirituality and theology: "All of Dutton's doctrinal, casuistical, experimental, and practical divinity, including her understanding of the spiritual journey, was grounded in Puritan divinity; she never wavered from it. The vast majority of her literary and theological influences were seventeenth century Puritans or her Puritan-inspired pastors of the early eighteenth century."[15] Their weight is captured by J. I. Packer's reverential depiction: "The mature holiness and seasoned fortitude of the great Puritans shine before us as a kind of beacon light, overtopping the stature of the majority of Christians in most eras."[16] Packer's explanation helps to unravel the remarkable honours heaped on Dutton from ages past:

> They were great souls serving a great God. In them clear-headed passion and warm-hearted compassion combined. Visionary and practical, idealistic and realistic too, goal-oriented and methodical, they were great believers, great hopers, great doers, and great sufferers. ... the Puritans' battles against the spiritual and climatic wildernesses in which God set them produced a virility of character, undaunted and unsinkable, rising above discouragement and fears.[17]

---

[14] Sciretti, "Feed My Lambs," 118.
[15] Sciretti, "Feed My Lambs," 117.
[16] J.I. Packer, *A Quest for Godliness: The Puritan Vision of the Christian Life* (Wheaton, Illinois: Crossway Books, 1990), 11.
[17] Packer, *Quest for Godliness*, 22.

The Spirituality of Anne Dutton

The landscape of Dutton's life and writings shows that she walked on a similar path, and just as the blazing legacy of the Puritans can nurture the lives of today's Christians, so too Dutton's.

Dutton's spiritual letters: wisdom borne from trial
The collected tone observed in Dutton's spiritual letters is the result of a journey through those "wildernesses" that Packer alludes to. Wise counsel expressed with godly conviction are characteristic of her correspondence. Letter upon letter, Dutton lovingly and conscientiously tended to these "lambs" (she felt called to especially care for those less seasoned in their faith), her words flowing from a heart that had similarly undergone intense spiritual struggle. This is most evident in her autobiography, its tenor and substance markedly different from her other writings. Her raw and honest personal account lays bare the fluctuations that exist in the Christian life and the journey involved in arriving at a firm assurance in Christ. For instance, once visited by a "very dangerous illness," Dutton describes the spiritual doubts that waged within her:

> Death stared me in the face. I thought myself just ready to launch into a vast eternity and knew not what would become of my poor soul. And now my distress rose high indeed! The waves and billows of God's apprehended wrath passed over me: I sunk in deep waters where there was no standing. Necessity was upon me: I must venture on Christ or perish; believe or die. And the conflict of my soul, between faith and unbelief, was exceeding great. Like a man a drowning, I catched at every twig; I laboured to take hold of the promises to keep me from sinking. But if I got a little support one moment, my innumerable transgressions, as so many weights, came pressing in upon me and sunk me the next. Oh, here lay the difficulty, to believe for myself in the face of so much sin and guilt! ... Christ Jesus, the hope of sinners, was in my view ... But oh, the weights which hung about me did much hinder my motion, the speediness of my flight![18]

---

[18] Watson, *Autobiography*, 18–19

Introduction

It was precisely this deep unrest, however, that eventually drove Dutton to rest securely in those promises she was so desperately seeking to take hold of. She opens her autobiography informing the reader that she had the benefit of a religious upbringing: her parents diligently taught her the gospel and doctrine, she attended public worship along with them, and she regularly engaged in private prayer as well as Bible reading and memorization. At times this led to her becoming a "proud, self-righteous creature" as she considered her religious "attainments" and felt she was "better than others."[19] At other times she felt her conscience "so tender" that she often faced temptations to doubt the Lord's love and felt assailed by the Enemy's lies and accusations. Dutton would tell of her experiences in finding refuge in the arms of Christ and then of the assaults: "…many were the combats I had with Satan and unbelief about my interest in the Lord Jesus."[20] Frequently her personal narrative reveals her wavering faith[21] before she fully believed that

> one direct act of faith on Christ or a fresh look to Jesus will bring more light and comfort to a distressed soul than a thousand looks into itself when the Spirit of God don't shine upon his own work. Especially if the soul makes conscience of taking God at his Word as to its having eternal life in believing on his Son. And it's a dreadful thing to make God a liar. We are all of us too much unacquainted with the abominable nature of unbelief as it gives the lie to infinite faithfulness.[22]

Only through this prolonged period of personal wrestling was Dutton in the position to speak authentically, attentively, and accurately into the lives of those who sought her counsel. But when she emerged, it was with remarkable force:

---

[19] Watson, *Autobiography*, 7.
[20] Watson, *Autobiography*, 24.
[21] "Fear and guilt alternated in her mind with joy and peace following the paradigm of piety dominant in the tradition extending from John Bunyan to John Wesley." Stein, "A Note on Anne Dutton," 486.
[22] Watson, *Autobiography*, 30–31.

The Spirituality of Anne Dutton

Dutton had learned not only to read her life like a text, but to use it like a text to preach a gospel message. She entered the rhetoric of conversion as a child, owned it and experienced it for herself, and then she offered it up as an exemplary life for others. Conversion was the axis upon which her life turned not only from sin to grace, but also from private experience to public expression and indeed public advocacy.[23]

Her spiritual writings would come to play an important part in the Evangelical Revival and among communities including the Calvinistic Baptists, Dissenters, Methodists, and American settlers. Welsh Methodist Howell Harris (1714–1773), for instance, recognized Dutton's writing ministry, stating to her that "Our Lord has entrusted you with a Talent of writing for him" and hoping that she would "live long to set forth with [her] Pen as public as possible, the Glory of that Grace."[24] Methodist preacher George Whitefield (1714–1770), in addition to his amicable correspondence with Dutton, would draw on her talent for the nurturing of believers in his own ministries: "I would have your correspondence enlarged, and therefore I set other people writing to you …"[25] Dutton would pen as many as twenty-two volumes of letters[26] to individuals, which she would then revise and publish for the spiritual edification of public readers.[27]

Dutton, further along in her spiritual walk, had arrived at a biblical view of God that enabled her to traverse the wildernesses with a steadfastness and courageousness that led to her accomplishing incredible

---

[23] D. Bruce Hindmarsh, *The Evangelical Conversion Narrative: Spiritual Autobiography in Early Modern England* (Oxford: Oxford University, 2005), 297.

[24] Stein, *A Note on Anne Dutton*, 488.

[25] George Whitefield to Anne Dutton, 13 October 1742, in *The Works of the Reverend George Whitefield*, edited by Gillies, I: p 450, qtd. in David Bebbington and David Ceri Jones's *Evangelicalism and Dissent in Modern England and Wales* (Abingdon, Oxon: Routledge, 2021), chapter 2 (see the section "Whitefield, Anne Dutton and the defence of Calvinistic Methodism" for a deeper picture of their relationship and collaboration).

[26] Michael Sciretti, "Anne Dutton as a Spiritual Director" (The Center for Christian Ethics at Baylor University, 2009), 31, https://www.baylor.edu/content/services/docment.php/98763.pdf.

[27] "the Lord gave me opportunity to write many letters to his dear lambs, who desired to hear from me. And I found my heart inclined to take the copies of them." Aug. 17, 1743. Watson, *Autobiography*, 213.

Introduction

work for the glory of Christ. To appreciate and learn from her pious example is to examine those wildernesses and observe how she responded to and grew from them. This is key because Christian spirituality is "lived doctrine": "Grace confers both gift and demand. God is love but, because his love is holy, spirituality must exhibit an ethical seriousness consistent with God's love and holiness."[28] The Christian life is therefore a response—committed and consequential—to a God who is worthy of all our worship. In the various wildernesses of Dutton's life, this "gift and demand" dynamic is evident in her autobiographical reflections and spiritual correspondence. A closer look at these wildernesses will reveal how doctrine shaped her character and informed her conduct in the events of her life.

The wilderness of sickness

Dutton battled with ill health throughout her life, suffering fevers, violent convulsions in the nerves, and weakness and pain in her body; at certain points, she was informed by physicians that she was verging on death.[29] But the gravity of her situation pointed her to an even graver one: "My body was filled with exquisite pain, but the agonies of my soul were a much greater distress."[30] She was made to see that worldly comforts were a threat to the real security that she needed, an unshakable assurance of her salvation:

> In all my former convictions, I was glad to get my trouble off and ease of conscience as soon as possible, but now I dreaded nothing more than that my concern should wear off without a saving conversion to Christ and the Lord himself speaking life and comfort to my soul. I knew that if I was left in a state of unbelief, to find ease and rest anywhere else than in the bosom of Christ, I must perish forever and therefore had a great dread of carnal security.[31]

---

[28] James M. Gordon, *Evangelical Spirituality* (Eugene, OR: Wipf & Stock Publishers, 1991), 3–4.
[29] Watson, *Autobiography*, 17–19.
[30] Watson, *Autobiography*, 18.
[31] Watson, *Autobiography*, 15.

The Spirituality of Anne Dutton

The unpredictability and frailty of her physical condition became trying seasons of learning to die to self and surrendering worldly comforts for a faith that, led by the Spirit, grew stronger as she kept on the great duty of taking God at his Word, not simply catching but clutching his life-giving promises. In this case, the promise was John 6:37, "Him that cometh to me I will in no wise cast out," a verse that appears repeatedly in her writings. Through God's powerful work in her, Dutton learned to trust—wholeheartedly—in his promises and unchanging character, even in "the face of ten thousand discouragements":

> This was a wonderful effect of omnipotent power and irresistible grace, which the power of unbelief was not able to withstand! Nothing less than the exceeding greatness of God's power could have raised up my soul from those depths of unbelieving fears to faith in Jesus! It was nothing less than an almighty voice that with one word of free grace could create peace in my troubled soul...[32]

Dutton's strengthened faith emerged out of physical trial, her assurance drawn from her Calvinist theology, and it would shape her spiritual journey until the end of her life. One historian describes how such theology nurtures the spiritual life: "Evangelicals articulate the heart of the struggle involved in seeking assurance: the seemingly calm and childlike trust is won only at great cost. Its positive fruit is a boldness before God which we have already seen to be characteristic of much Calvinist piety."[33]

Dutton's boldness is seen, for example, in how she continually counseled individuals who were suffering from "soul-diseases," those who struggled to sense God's favour and feel the comfort of his presence, her striking tenderness toward them springing from one who had personally grappled with those very weaknesses. Her epistolary ministry in this area would culminate in her three letters *Marks of a Child of*

---

[32] Watson, *Autobiography*, 19.
[33] Gordon Mursell, *English Spirituality: From 1700 to the Present Day* (London: SPCK, 2001), 26. Mursell examines eighteenth-century English spirituality; for Calvinists, he studies the life of George Whitefield and John Newton.

Introduction

God, Soul-Diseases of God's Children, and *God's Prohibition of his People's Unbelieving Fear,* published only years before her death. In its conclusion, her advice to ministers of Christ (who were directing believers to observe these marks in their lives) displays her acquired sensitivity:

> A great piece of spiritual wisdom it is in a minister of Christ, thus to direct Christians to seek for these marks of their being the children of God from their proper springs and at their proper times. And so of Christian prudence to seek for marks of grace when they *were* or *are* in the exercise of grace. Else, a minister of Christ will rather wound than help the faith of Christians. And a true believer, by unbelief, will enter through the gate of seen and felt carnality into an endless maze of doubt and perplexity concerning his spirituality and so of his being a child of God truly.

Only a child of God, her theology informs, can experience any stirring of the Holy Spirit:

> It is sufficient to prove any one to be such if he ever hath found or doth find in him these marks of grace when he was or is under divine influence and in the exercise of grace. For none but God's children are ever thus wrought upon.[34]

Dutton, ailing and confronting her mortality, was set in a wilderness that moved her to seek an unyielding assurance of God's saving work in her life, which would later prepare her to guide others who felt lost.

This was not the only fruit that came from Dutton's suffering of ill health. It also moved her to solemnly ponder how she ought to redeem her time on earth. Her outlook reflected that of the Puritans who, living amid the realities of pain and death in the seventeenth-century, learned "to regard readiness to die as the first step in learning to live," aware that they were "just one step from eternity," and this "gave them a deep

---

[34] Anne Dutton, *Three Letters on I. The Marks of a Child of God. II. The Soul-Diseases of God's Children; and their Soul-Remedies. And III. God's Prohibition of His People's Unbelieving Fear...* (London: J. Hart, 1761), 10.

The Spirituality of Anne Dutton

seriousness, calm yet passionate, with regard to the business of living."[35] Writing at one point when she was near the "gates of death," Dutton expressed her readiness to die yet also her regret:

> And in the faith of God's everlasting kindness and that glory he had prepared for me, I could freely have gone home. But in the review of my past life, while I looked back upon the Lord's wonderful goodness towards me and all the great things he had done for me, I was much grieved that I had done so little for him.

The looming reality of death ignited her intense yearning to serve her Lord well—with diligence and gratitude:

> I was wonderfully favoured with overcoming discoveries of God's love, and had sweet peace with him in the faith of his passing by all my transgressions; but this pierced my heart, that my dear Father had had so little glory by me in an active way.

Prayerfully, in humble submission, Dutton petitioned her Lord for more time that she might offer her life as a living sacrifice for his glory:

> I knew that I should glorify him perfectly when I came to heaven, but then I thought I should not have the opportunity of glorifying him before men as I might have while in the body. And my heart being much drawn out in desires to do something for God before I was taken home to the full enjoyment of him, I asked this favour of the Lord, "That, if consistent with his eternal purpose, he would spare my life a little longer and that the whole of my remaining days, under the influence of his own Spirit, might be cast as a drop of service into the ocean of his love..."[36]

She would live another two decades.

Dutton, of course, enjoyed receiving letters from individuals expressing how they were encouraged by her counsel, "I have read [your

---
[35] Packer, *A Quest for Godliness*, 13–14.
[36] Watson, *Autobiography*, 135–136.

Introduction

last letter] again and again with tears of joyful wonder at the infinite grace of God to vile, unworthy me in making my poor books of such blessed use to you to bring you to Jesus and to build you up in him,"[37] this being a natural fuel for her industrious letter writing. But her task, at points, also involved the fatiguing act of re-copying letters, and it was with her eye on God's glory that she was willing to toil. Further, she revealed that illness once caused her to neglect her work, but once again, the acute sense of her life being provisional compelled her to keep at it:

> If the time of my dissolution was near, what would I do for Christ before I am taken up to be forever with the Lord? And that Word was brought to my mind, "Well done thou good and faithful servant; enter thou into the joy of the Lord." And instantly, glancing upon that work which I had left undone, [I] thought, "That my Lord could not call me 'good and faithful servant'" because I had neglected doing that which he set me about.

After "[bewailing her] negligence," Dutton felt the kind Lord calling her "to engage afresh in the work" which she "had so long neglected."[38] When a recovery enabled her to be carried "comfortably through the work," she attributed her physical and spiritual strengthening to her Lord's good and sovereign timing.[39] What Packer esteemed of the Puritans was also true for Dutton: "Reckoning with death brought appreciation of each day's continued life, and the knowledge that God would eventually decide, without consulting them, when their work on earth was done brought energy for the work itself while they were still being given time to get on with it."[40] In her delicate condition, Dutton had regarded her life like that of the apostle Paul, to live was to glorify Christ and to die was to enter into his glorious presence.

---

[37] Dutton, *Letters on Spiritual Subjects*, 64, Letter XVII, To Mrs. H-----ys.
[38] Watson, *Autobiography*, 217.
[39] Watson, *Autobiography*, 218
[40] Packer, *A Quest for Godliness*, 14.

The wilderness of being away from Christ-centred worship

Another repeated trial that Dutton felt acutely was the possibility of being removed from the gospel ministries of beloved pastors. Different circumstances prompted a change in worship settings throughout her life. Her first marriage at age 22 meant moving away from her pastor Mr. Moore, who was a "great doctrinal preacher," and her church, with whom she walked "comfortably" and whose communion was "pleasant."[41] This initial change, it turned out, brought on an even richer ministry with Mr. Skepp, a preacher who taught her doctrinal truths with even greater "life and power" because of his gifts of, among many, expounding the Scriptures, drawing out heavenly realities through compelling illustration, and enlivening the souls of the saints and convicting sinners: "I found the gospel under his preaching to be indeed the ministration of the Spirit and life, and the Word of God to be as a fire melting my soul down. Oh, the light and glory I saw, the life and heat I felt in the doctrines of the gospel under the irradiating, enkindling influences of the Holy Ghost in his ministry!"[42]

Dutton relished in being in a Christ-centered church in which she was continually fed and nurtured. When her husband's business called for them to locate elsewhere and she was deprived of this, she despaired and did not hold back her judgment on that church: "I found a strange alteration: I was got into another climate, much further off the sun. I thought, when I came first, 'Surely this people worship *without* the blood of Jesus.' They stood at such a distance from God in prayer; and as for preaching, I thought it little more than form."[43] For Dutton, partaking in biblical public worship was a central means of meeting God; her attendance was as much an expression of obedience as it was an intense personal need and profound joy. When illness or the death of a pastor threatened to take away her experience of faithful preaching, she grieved: "For I longed for the water of life through *that* channel, but

---

[41] Watson, *Autobiography*, 50.
[42] Watson, *Autobiography*, 51.
[43] Watson, *Autobiography*, 55.

Introduction

when the pipe was broke and no hope left of my hearing him anymore, I was full of heaviness."[44]

Likewise, when the weakness of her own physical condition prevented her from meeting in God's house for weeks (on one occasion, she noted it was "nine Lord's Days"), she felt it a difficult trial to endure, referring to such times as her "captivity" or "affliction chains" and her return as a restoration of those "privileges."[45] Worshipping alongside the body of Christ was among them, for it was a taste of the future glory: "If the saints fellowship in the spirit of grace, which yet is increasing, by that which every joint supplieth, has such a ravishing sweetness and spiritual glory in it—what will be their fellowship in heaven when the whole mystical body shall be complete, and the Spirit of glory from Christ the head shall fill every member of the body!"[46] The picture she saw of worship was of a glorious feast at the King's table and she mourned when she was kept back from partaking in it. On an earlier occasion, upon recovering from illness, she had discovered a new appreciation for the private means of grace and public ordinances:

> The Lord raised me up from a sick-bed from death to life, both in soul and body. I was, as it were, brought forth into a new world: all things appeared new to me... Religious duties were now very precious to me, such as hearing, reading, praying, meditation, and converse with Christians; and much of God I enjoyed in them. The saints were now my own company: I esteemed them, the excellent of the earth in whom was all my delight. Lord's days were the joy of my heart, Sabbaths indeed to me.[47]

In experiencing the deprivations of Christ-exalted preaching and a Christian community, Dutton unearthed a more profound pleasure in private and public worship, which she would describe in *Walking with God* as God's "infinite condescension": "Will he that is far above all

---

[44] Watson, *Autobiography*, 66, 138.
[45] Watson, *Autobiography*, 133.
[46] Watson, *Autobiography*, 72.
[47] Watson, *Autobiography*, 22–23.

blessing and praise,[48] that humbleth himself to behold the worship of heaven,[49] yet bow down a gracious ear to the chattering prayers and praises of mortal, sinful men whose foundation is in the dust!"[50] Humbled that it was Christ who made divine worship possible, she duly felt her participation an honour—and one she could not bear to be without.

The wilderness of self-doubt and insecurity

The sheer magnitude of Dutton's spiritual writings becomes even more remarkable considering the fears and doubts she had battled. Of course, Dutton possessed a passion to serve her Lord with her pen, but this was attended by her natural sense of "unworthiness, weakness, and unfitness for his service."[51] Engaging in the work was spiritual warfare. Dampening her will to continue were disheartening thoughts —that her work would be fruitless and done in vain (they would never be printed);[52] that she was a sinner and unworthy of writing about such gloriously divine subjects;[53] that her intentions were tainted by external motives;[54] that other servants worthier than she could produce more valuable work;[55] and that it was doubtful her Lord could delight in the work of "such an unlovely creature."[56] At one point Dutton admitted that she had been "in great distress…for above a year" and "was ready to give all up."[57] Many a moment, simultaneous was her desire to write and her dismay at the task at hand: "I feared my God was displeased with me for not improving those present moments which he gave me for that service… There was at times a desire on my heart after the work, but I sometimes found I had lost my spirit for it and often feared

---

[48] Nehemiah 9:5
[49] Psalm 113:6.
[50] Anne Dutton, *A Discourse upon Walking with God: In a Letter to a Friend…* (London: Printed for the author and sold by E. Gardner, 1735), 33.
[51] Watson, *Autobiography*, 135.
[52] Watson, *Autobiography*, 161.
[53] Watson, *Autobiography*, 187.
[54] Watson, *Autobiography*, 174.
[55] Watson, *Autobiography*, 175.
[56] Watson, *Autobiography*, 185.
[57] Watson, *Autobiography*, 195.

Introduction

that it would be useless if I then attempted it."[58] This inner wilderness of writing while struggling to feel confident in the process and results led Dutton to look to God for deliverance.

Out of weakness she prayed. Whenever she felt that her work was inadequate or insubstantial, she fled to "the God of all grace for all the supplies [she] needed for his service."[59] She knew she needed God to plant in her both the desire to serve him and the ability—on him she wholly depended, and so she petitioned for a "heart to serve him" and a "hand too," knowing that "free grace must empty me, incline me, and assist me, or I could do nothing."[60] Drawing from the Lord her provider rather than lamenting her "own barrenness," Dutton learned to be grateful "for every kind and degree of fruitfulness" that she had been given.[61]

And with however "little" she had, she trusted that her faithful God could do much.[62] Whatever became of her was no matter if God could use "so little a worm" to serve the saints and glorify himself; in fact, he would be more glorified.[63] Dutton compared herself to the widow who cast in her two mites: "It is my all, my heart is in it; it is all that I can do for my Lord,"[64] and so she proceeded, "I offered up a mite, all my soul could give in the name of Jesus."[65] Her work was her spiritual offering; she took God at his Word that it was acceptable (on her heart was 1 Cor. 15:58). Her purpose was to direct sinners to Christ, and so it did not matter how it fared with her, whether others more honourable than she outshined her or whether she would be judged for it. Duty superseded her doubts: "…in the Lord's name and strength, I began the work."[66] This also explains how Dutton's boldness and tenacity

---

[58] Watson, *Autobiography*, 217.
[59] Watson, *Autobiography*, 149.
[60] Watson, *Autobiography*, 149.
[61] Watson, *Autobiography*, 154.
[62] Watson, *Autobiography*, 170.
[63] Watson, *Autobiography*, 174–175. In Dutton's words, "The Lord showed me that the weaker the instrument was that attempted his service, the more himself, the Almighty agent, would be glorified in working by it." Watson, *Anne Dutton Autobiography*, 209.
[64] Watson, *Autobiography*, 175.
[65] Watson, *Autobiography*, 198.
[66] Watson, *Autobiography*, 217.

The Spirituality of Anne Dutton

emerged despite her vacillations—authoring lengthy instructive expositions on profound subjects such as *Walking with God*[67] and *Duty of Love*[68] and correcting perceived theological error (which could incite censure)[69]: "it is the will of my Lord that I should write it, and necessity is laid upon me to do so."[70] Her writing was as much calling and duty as it was responsibility to uphold truth: the Lord's words—"My truth is valuable: wilt thou not speak it?"[71]—resounded in her conscience.

Finally, the awareness that she was a sinner writing on spiritual subjects, unworthy of the mission, inviting the charge of hypocrite for her attempts, was silenced by one truth: "But in the views of Christ's blood cleansing me, and my performances from all sin, and of his presenting them acceptable to the Father in his own perfections, I have got the victory over this."[72] Whenever her insecurities welled up, Christ had the final word: "I saw that Christ loved me and that in love to my person he accepted my offering, my service, my feeble work!"[73] This, in fact, exacted a greater impetus to perform her duty: "I am washed in Christ's blood and forgiven by free grace, and therefore under the greater obligation to publish its praises."[74] Basking in a "life full of mercies, of supports, comforts, deliverances, of marvellous salvations, and amazing favours,"[75] Dutton proclaiming them was merely an outflow of her worship.

---

[67] Of this work, she writes: "Days should speak and multitudes of years should teach that wisdom and not such a babe as I." Watson, *Autobiography*, 162.

[68] Dutton's concern about penning *Duty of Love* was "that it would rise up in judgment against me and condemn me by reason of my little love to them, and therefore I had better desist and say nothing about it." Watson, *Autobiography*, 187.

[69] Dutton clarifies her position: "I don't natively delight in controversy; the prospect of it was not naturally pleasing to me. But upon my receiving his little corrupt piece, fitted to entangle souls, the Lord said unto me, 'Rise up my love, my fair one, and come away.'" Watson, *Autobiography*, 223.

[70] Watson, *Autobiography*, 187.

[71] From Jeremiah 23:28. Watson, *Autobiography*, 219.

[72] Watson, *Autobiography*, 175.

[73] Watson, *Autobiography*, 200.

[74] Watson, *Autobiography*, 175.

[75] Watson, *Autobiography*, 181.

Introduction

The wilderness of facing opposition and criticism

Dutton's oft-referenced tract published in 1743, "To such of the Servants of Christ, who have any Scruple about the Lawfulness of PRINTING any Thing written by a Woman," which lays out her biblical defence against objections to her publishing,[76] might lead us to overlook the wilderness she trudged through facing well-meaning Christians who challenged her radical decision to do so.[77] Dutton felt it greatly herself: "another objection arose in my mind from the weakness of my sex, which, together with my personal weakness, did greatly tend to discourage my hopes of doing any service to the cause of Christ."[78] The adverse response from the public made that wilderness deeper and darker: "some slighted and despised me, which was one cause of my dejection and made me fear that I should be no more useful,"[79] especially when it came from those dearer to her, "I received a letter from a friend, the contents whereof proved very trying. And I was much dejected, fearing the Lord would cast me off as to usefulness."[80]

Since her aim was to be fruitful, the unwelcoming reception made her question her efforts. This became a season of testing: "When I received another letter from a friend, and by some things in it which I

---

[76] Regarding whether she had the biblical authority to teach, Dutton argued that since writing is received "in the private house of another person," it is not "public," that is, not exercising the "public authority of Christ in his Church," as in preaching. Watson, *Autobiography*, 255.

For a summary and discussion of this tract, see Michael A.G. Haykin, "English Calvinistic Baptists and Vocation in the Long Eighteenth Century, with Particular Reference to Anne Dutton's Calling as an Author." The Southern Baptist Journal of Theology 22.1 (2018): 80–81.

Sciretti captures Dutton's view of her role in the church: "The familial basis of her spiritual direction ministry served as a theological reason why she freely corresponded with evangelical leaders. ... In the body of Christ there is only one 'Head,' Jesus, and in the family of God there is only one 'Father,' God. All believers therefore are equal brothers and sisters. Dutton took this theology seriously, and as a spiritual guide she related to counselees as an elder sister guiding the younger 'Babes' who were ignorant or forgetful of the contours of the Christian pilgrimage." Sciretti, "Anne Dutton as a Spiritual Director" (Waco, TX: The Center for Christian Ethics at Baylor University, 2009), 32.

[77] "Conventions dictated that women refrain from writing for the public on religious topics. Offenders faced opposition and resistance. ... Even the evangelical party with its grant of spiritual equality to male and female alike was no different." While Howell Harris esteemed Dutton for her spiritual writings, he knew it would not be easy for her to find keen readers. Stein, *A Note on Anne Dutton*, 488.

[78] Watson, *Autobiography*, 145.

[79] Watson, *Autobiography*, 167.

[80] Sept. 1741. Watson, *Autobiography*, 177.

The Spirituality of Anne Dutton

thought looked as if they would hinder my usefulness, I was somewhat oppressed in spirit for a time."[81] Feeling disparaged, she described this trial in the early forties as her "darkest dispensation"[82]: "I had a desire kept up in my soul to glorify him, although as to the present appearance of things, I seemed to be cast out of his sight, and was apt to say, at times, with the Church, my strength and my hope (as to usefulness) is perished from the Lord (Lam. 3:18)."[83] Her circumstances escalated to such a grave degree that she thought, "the Lord would not let [me][84] in the world long when my work for him seemed to be done."[85] When opposition eventually drove her printed works out of England, Dutton saw this as the devil pursuing and persecuting the woman and that "friends of Christ" had become "channels of his rage."[86] Behind that essay of defence was a woman who sought to overcome the crushing indignation of dear saints in Christ.

Scripture was her consolation. Dutton was heartened by women whom God used for his glorious service, like Miriam (Micah 6:4)[87] and Priscilla (Acts 18:26).[88] The seemingly bleak situation of Abraham and Sarah before Isaac's birth granted her hope that her Lord would deal similarly with her: "That though all within and without me seemed to be dead, and no appearance of fruitfulness, yet that by the force of the promise I should be enabled to bring forth fruit unto God."[89] Forsaken by certain friends, Dutton found unbroken fellowship with the one faithful friend: "whoever might not desire communion with me, Christ would."[90] "Christ and his love," in her loneliness, was "very precious" to her soul, and this revived her spirit: "My heart melted into tears of

---

[81] Oct. 1741. Watson, *Autobiography*, 177.
[82] Watson, *Autobiography*, 178.
[83] Watson, *Autobiography*, 178–179.
[84] "me" corrected from "be."
[85] Watson, *Autobiography*, 165.
[86] Revelation 12. Watson, *Autobiography*, 205.
[87] Watson, *Autobiography*, 145.
[88] Watson, *Autobiography*, 255.
[89] Watson, *Autobiography*, 166.
[90] Watson, *Autobiography*, 177.

Introduction

joy and humility."⁹¹ "My beloved is mine, and I am his" (Song 2:16) was the cry of this needy soul.

Trust in a sovereign God emboldened her. Since Dutton's labours were for the glory of Christ, she could be confident that they would not return empty: "if the Lord shut up one way of glorifying of him, he would open another," fruit being borne in her own life—"that if I might not glorify him by usefulness to others, I might inwardly and secretly, in my own soul, glorify him more abundantly than ever."⁹² How people received her writing was out of her control, and this reality steered her into surrender: "as things at present seemed to work against me, I found a desire to make an entire resignation of myself and my dearest interest in being useful to souls to the Lord's sovereign disposal (1 Sam. 15:22)."⁹³

Not witnessing evidence of the fruit of her labours was disappointing. Yet when news did come, she felt it was her Lord's timing, having "brought it to my view when I had most need of the consolation."⁹⁴ Letters of criticism arrived, but so too those of gratitude. Immensely blessed felt she to hear that her books edified and comforted "our dear Lord's tender lambs." Amid a cloud of condemnation, Dutton saw it "a very great mercy" that a "remnant which the Lord left me here" in England had expressed their appreciation of her books.⁹⁵ One woman wrote to her about being converted after reading the first volume of her letters; Dutton saw it as God's providence and affirmation of her ministry.⁹⁶ When her books bore fruit in America, she felt her blessing magnified: "God sent them beyond the seas, wrought marvels by his mighty hand for their disposal…"⁹⁷ The bitter became sweet as God's Word enabled her to see his good purpose in her trial: "things which are despised hath God chosen (1 Cor. 1:28). I have thought, 'It was in some

---

⁹¹ Watson, *Autobiography*, 177.
⁹² Watson, *Autobiography*, 177.
⁹³ "disposal" corrected from "dispose." Watson, *Autobiography*, 177.
⁹⁴ Watson, *Autobiography*, 237.
⁹⁵ Watson, *Autobiography*, 167.
⁹⁶ Watson, *Autobiography*, 195.
⁹⁷ Watson, *Autobiography*, 167.

respect needful that I should be despised, that the grace of God in using me might be the more conspicuous.'"[98]

In such a wilderness Dutton saw the Lord's care for her, from which she drew lessons for other believers:

> Let the dear saints be cautious when God applies promises to comfort them in their distresses which foretell their deliverances, how they draw out ways and fix times for God to walk and work in. As he often performs his Word, answers their faith and prayer, fulfills and even exceeds their desires in granting them not those very things or not in those very ways which they most earnestly wish and expect but in others, which for his glory and their good, are far, far better.[99]

The wilderness of loss

No more than five years after marrying Thomas Cattell in 1715, Dutton recorded that "it pleased the Lord to take away my yokefellow by death."[100] Around a year or so later, she met and married her second husband Benjamin Dutton; but, sadly, upon Mr. Dutton's return home from America in 1747, she recorded that "it pleased God to exercise me with so great a trial as the loss of my dear husband by sea."[101] In both accounts, reminiscent of the first chapter of Job, Dutton recognized God's sovereignty over her life—though this did not diminish her anguish. First time widowed, she wrote that the ordeal was "trying" and "very dark" and that her heart was "troubled." While submitting to God's will, Dutton could at the same time admit, "I was in some measure quieted under the hand of God, ashamed of my peevish carriage under the rod and thought well of what He had done."[102]

Having endured much more hardship by the time she entered widowhood again in her fifties, Dutton still weighed the trial of mourning

---

[98] Watson, *Autobiography*, 167.
[99] Watson, *Autobiography*, 248.
[100] Watson, *Autobiography*, 63.
[101] Watson, *Autobiography*, 238.
[102] Watson, *Autobiography*, 63–64.

Introduction

her second husband's death as "the greatest I ever met with."[103] She had faced repeated blows of disappointment while awaiting his return, and news of the foundering ship seemed to be a "denial of [her] earnest prayers," which she had hoped would be included in "God's never-failing promises." She could see no other outcome other than what she had hoped for: "fain, very fain,[104] would I have seen the promises fulfilled in my dear husband's safe return and his abundant usefulness. I could see no way like this for the glory of God and our joy."[105] This widow's unfolding revelations of her emotional agony leads us to appreciate even more her eventual deliverance, especially since Mr. Dutton's absence was not her only distress. Great Gransden had lost a beloved shepherd: "Their desolate case made my heart desolate."[106] Even more injurious, critics of Dutton's writing ministry interpreted her husband's death as divine rebuke (Mr. Dutton had decided on his own initiative to bring some of his wife's books with him to America to minister to souls alongside his own ministry). With these griefs coming at her all at once during her darkest hour, Dutton's response reveals much about her godly character.

This widow felt God's face hidden from her during her suffering, yet she trusted that she would in due time "behold his righteousness."[107] Her lamenting was attended by a resignation to her Heavenly Father's will: "Whatever my God doth with me, he will be glorified and that shall be my joy."[108] Grateful was she that her husband had not only reached America to distribute her books abroad but that he was also able to notify her of their spiritual fruit. An even greater consolation was her husband's humbled and awestruck report of how God used his ministry to convert as many as 11 or 12 souls:

---

[103] Watson, *Autobiography*, 243.
[104] Meaning, "Glad; merry; cheerful; fond." Johnson, Samuel. "fain." *A Dictionary of the English Language*, https://johnsonsdictionaryonline.com/1755/fain_adj, 1755. Accessed May 27, 2023.
[105] Watson, *Autobiography*, 241.
[106] Watson, *Autobiography*, 240.
[107] Watson, *Autobiography*, 239.
[108] Watson, *Autobiography*, 239.

> And this was to me a very great joy and made the pain of absence more easy. Yea, I thought, when I had this news, "That I could freely give him up to the Lord's service if he should call for his very life to be spent in it and that I should lose my pain for his absence in the pleasure of my Lord's glory…"[109]

In reading her husband's letters about the outcome of his ministry as well as her writing, Dutton came to see more profoundly the outworking of God's wisdom and grace in adversity: "sweetly the Lord drew me into resignation to and acquiescence with his good pleasure."[110] The temptations to doubt and sink into despair were keenly felt, but she was mightily supported: "The Lord in tender pity restrained the power of darkness and blessed me with the light of promise that I might endure the gloom of providence." Envisioning God's sovereign work lifted her out of sorrow and strengthened her for obedience: "Meanwhile, to give my God a little glory by the trial, oh, it was joy in sorrow, ease in pain, life in death to my spirit!"[111] In her weeping arose a deepened faith that glorified her God.

Confronting her critics, Dutton did not stagger, standing firmly on her biblical understanding of God's character. The God of Job was hers as well, and so her defence, "Great trials are not always the fruit of great sins, nor a token of God's great displeasure." No one can claim to fully know the mind of God and his ways and is therefore in no position to pronounce judgment on her situation. In the face of her accusers, Dutton responded with grace, explaining that God's "various dispensations towards his dear children is not to be taken merely from the outward face of things in providence but rather from the inward effect of those dispensations upon their souls."[112] In her case, she felt assured of the Lord's mercy in her circumstances and testified to that end.

---

[109] Watson, *Autobiography*, 240.
[110] Watson, *Autobiography*, 240.
[111] Watson, *Autobiography*, 243.
[112] Watson, *Autobiography*, 238.

Introduction

Dutton's views in the wilderness

In her journey through these arduous wildernesses, Dutton was guided by a particularly keen understanding of God and the Christian life that enabled her to not only endure trial but to do so faithfully. Her views while being in the thick of these wildernesses prove instructive for readers today.

In *Walking with God*, Dutton distinguishes between two kinds of believers, one who relies heavily on immediately visible manifestations of God's graces for their comfort and assurance (she refers to these as "the props of spiritual sense"), that is, self-sufficiency, duty, and God's wonderful blessings; and one who trusts first and foremost in Christ as promised by the Word and attested by the Spirit. She was sensitive to these varying degrees of maturity among believers yet entreated all to walk by faith, even when without the "light of spiritual sense."[113] Her own trials certainly put her through this journey. Such blessings as health, public worship, support of her gifts and calling, and safety of her loved ones were stripped away from her. But in her utter neediness she learned increasingly to walk with God without dependence on sight, such that she could make such declarations:

> It's well for us that there is something more stable than our own frames to rejoice in.[114]

---

[113] Consider what Dutton writes in her letter *The Soul-Diseases of God's Children and their Soul-Remedies*: "At first conversion, and while God eminently shines upon his dear children, they are apt to live too much by *spiritual sense*. As to taking up their faith of interest in Christ, principally from the secondary evidence of their graces rather than from the prime evidence thereof, the faithfulness of God in his promise-Word, which secures and declares to every soul that believes in Jesus upon its first act of faith an entire and eternal interest in him unto a full and everlasting salvation by him. And while they thus live by sense, they can believe no longer than they see.

Again, a culpable life of sense is trusting in our inherent beauty and going forth in duty, as it were, in self-sufficiency, and in idolizing God's fair jewels, our given graces.

When this therefore is the case with God's favourites, he stretcheth out his hand over them and diminisheth their ordinary food and gives them up, as it were, for a time into the hand of them that hate them, who strip them of their clothes, take away their fair jewels, and leave them naked and bare." Dutton, *Three Letters on 1. The Marks of a Child of God. II. The Soul-Diseases of God's Children; ...III. God's Prohibition of His People's Unbelieving Fear: ...By One Who Has Tasted that the Lord is Gracious* (London: Printed by J. Hart, in Popping's-Court, Fleet-Street, 1761), 16.

[114] Watson, *Autobiography*, 116.

> God's continual walking with us is our safety, the faith of it our comfort.[115]

> I had indeed some interruptions of communion; but in those intervals, I was made by an efficacious Word of power to stand fast by faith in that liberty wherewith Christ had made me free (Gal. 5:1) when I had not spiritual sensation, being rooted and grounded in love (Eph. 3:17).[116]

Not staking her confidence in herself or the continual bestowal of God's more tangible graces, Dutton was induced to draw her hope from a steadfast source that granted her a stunning strength to submit to her Lord and bear her suffering.

Dutton's awareness of the different seasons of the Christian life also helped her to persevere amidst privations. She held fast to God's promises, mindful that their fulfillment was according to his sovereign design:

> But as I was looking upon the trees in the garden, it being winter-season, the Lord was pleased to instruct me from thence. That as it was winter with the garden, so now it was the winter-season with respect to the promise, and that it was as unreasonable for me to conclude that there would never be a spring time of the promise because I saw no appearance of it as it would be to think that there should never be a natural spring because the trees in winter look so much like dead ones.[117]

Bleak as her condition or circumstances could be, she recognized that the sight of her present landscape was not an indication of her standing with God. Traveling through those tortuous wildernesses—wandering or plodding at times—Dutton could envision a forthcoming brilliantly lit treescape of vibrant blossoms. This vision sprang from her biblically

---

[115] Dutton, *Walking with God*, 64.
[116] Dutton, *Walking with God*, 163–164.
[117] Watson, *Autobiography*, 85.

Introduction

grounded view of God: the warmth in her winter was "a distinct view of [God] being [her] tender, wise, strong, and faithful friend,"[118] and "it was the views of him as [her] own gracious God and Father that made [her] submit to his wisdom if he should cross [hers]."[119] Should her vision be shadowed by the biting frost of present pain, Dutton would recall earlier comforts: "I had a glorious view of the Lord's past appearances for me, and that he was the same in his grace, power, and faithfulness now as he was then."[120] God's treasured Word would be accomplished—in time, manner, and degree—according to his heavenly mind and heart for her, and this discernment directed her faith: "being satisfied about the sureness of the promised mercy, I was resigned into God's will as to the time of it, believing that he would bring it forth in its proper season in which it should appear most beautiful."[121] As a result, she came to see the grace that was present in all the spiritual seasons of her life:

> Sometimes *he helps me* to trust him, sometimes to wait for him, and at other times vehemently to long for him, even to a kind of fainting or love-sickness, and sometimes I am quite the reverse to all these. But yet *the Lord gives me* gracious hints that he will come. And when I hadn't that assurance, yet *he leads me* into the depths of my own wants and distresses and *makes the declarations and promises of his grace*, together with his dealings with his people in such circumstances, to be very sweet to me; and *I am helped* to cast myself upon the grace which shines forth in all these, *to be dealt with* accordingly.[122] (emphasis mine)

Dutton knew the Lord was present with her—however intimately she was experiencing that divine communion. Wherever she trekked, whatever turns and trails she took, in the cold or warmth, in the

---

[118] Watson, *Autobiography*, 125.
[119] Watson, *Autobiography*, 83.
[120] Watson, *Autobiography*, 124.
[121] Watson, *Autobiography*, 76.
[122] Watson, *Autobiography*, 125.

dimness or light, the Lord was ahead of her, his promised grace her trusted guide.

Dutton's view of biblical love

The discussion of Dutton's piety, however, cannot end here. Christian spirituality is not only about how a believer expresses his or her love to God—but also to neighbour (Matt. 22:36–40), "Love to God and our neighbour is the sum of our duty."[123] Of course, Dutton's substantial correspondence is already a resounding testimony of her love to neighbour. A survey of her letters shows her compassionate and empathetic response to individuals concerning their struggles. A letter excerpt reveals Dutton's profound affection for fellow saints and her tender welcome to them to share with her their burdens:

> It is our Privilege, a Part of the Communion of Saints, to unbosom our Souls to each other, to bear each other's Burdens, to see each other's Good, to rejoice with them that rejoice, and to mourn with them that mourn. The more *free* you are with me, the more *kindly* I take it, the more my Spirit runs into yours, and interests itself in your Concerns. God grant me a Bosom large enough, to embrace all his Children, and to receive all their Cases with the greatest Sympathy![124]

How marvellously did the Lord answer this devout writer's prayer. We have already seen her incredible sacrifice of time and energy for and sensitivity to the more vulnerable among the body of Christ.

To factor in *A Letter to All the Saints on the General Duty of Love*, which was published in Dutton's early fifties, is merely to add final brushstrokes to an already breathtaking canvas. Earnestness and insistence permeate her appeal to believers to love one another. But her message was not at all simplistic. The letter demonstrates her biblically rich

---

[123] Anne Dutton, *A Letter to All the Saints on the General Duty of Love: Humbly Presented, by One That is Less Than the Least of Them All, and Unworthy to be of Their Happy Number* (London: Printed by John Hart and sold by J. Lewis and E. Gardner, 1743), 4.

[124] Sciretti, "Feed my Lambs," 342. In a Letter from Anne Dutton to Rev. Jonathan Barber (*Letters, Volume III*).

Introduction

understanding of putting love into action as she lays out its theological grounds, spectrum of applications, and purposes. In so doing, Dutton depicts for readers her own desired path, her holy aspirations: "I write it as a rule to myself as well as others. And as to teach others and not do the same things myself is an aggravated sin, so I desire to watch and that hereby I may be the more quickened to the obedience of love."[125]

In retrospect, love ultimately shone in all of Dutton's wildernesses: in the wilderness of sickness, her love for the weak in faith; in the wilderness without public worship, her love for fellowshipping with the saints; in the wilderness of self-doubt, opposition, and loss, her love for the salvation and edification of souls. "Love is as it were the very essence of a Christian, of Christianity in his soul,"[126] wrote Dutton, and this collection of letters shall attest to her life's conviction.

Selected letters of Anne Dutton in this collection

The following collection of letters is organized into three parts. The first and third parts comprise excerpts from Dutton's extensive treatments of two vital subjects: "the first principles of the mystery of walking with God"[127] and the believer's duty to demonstrate "love to the saints." The two works, in effect, attest to the depth of Dutton's character and spirituality.

Due to their lengths (*Walking with God* totalling about 36,000 words and *Duty of Love* 13,000 words), presenting these works in their entirety is not feasible. Yet, to only present particular sections from these letters at the expense of others would be to overlook the writer's comprehensive examination of these central Christian themes. In *Walking with God*, for example, how can we read Dutton's discussion of why we can freely and intimately walk with God ("for in Christ Jesus we stand in a nearer relation to God than angels") without also reading her account of the way in which this reality is observed in the Christian life (by our faith, worship, experience of God's providence, and holy

---

[125] Watson, *Autobiography*, 187.
[126] Dutton, *Duty of Love*, 44.
[127] Dutton, *Walking with God*, 4.

living)? Or, in *Duty of Love*, how can we read all the grounds for why we ought to love the saints yet not also read all the ways Dutton counsels the Christian to love (through our compassion for one another's sin and suffering, forbearance with each other's differences, pursuit of one another's happiness and good, and celebration—without envy— of one another's blessings)? The counsel provided in these two works is valuable precisely because of her scrupulous treatment of the subjects. Each work—with the sum of its parts—offers a rich portrayal of the writer's vision of the Christian life, which Dutton, as we have seen, faithfully applied to her own.

Hence, Part I of this book provides a cross-section of *Walking with God* and Part III provides a cross-section of *Duty of Love*—that is, excerpts are taken from every section of each of the works. The excerpts are presented in a format that allows for them to be appreciated individually so they can be meditated on one at a time. While the subtitles in these works are Dutton's, additional paragraphing has been incorporated to signify a movement in thought. The excerpts represent key ideas in each section, allowing readers to grasp the overall arc of each work.

Walking with God and *Duty of Love* are meant to serve as bookends: it seems fitting to begin this collection with Dutton's biblically grounded insight into what characterizes the Christian walk and to conclude the collection with what she characterizes as the outward expression of that walk.

Part II, then, offers an interlude between these two larger works. It comprises 10 letters selected from *Letters on Spiritual Subjects and Diverse Occasions; sent to Relations and Friends*. This 1747 publication includes a total of 44 private letters Dutton wrote to particular individuals or groups, some letters numbering hundreds of words and some thousands.[128] Some of these longer letters have been included in this selection, and where they have been condensed, an ellipsis indicates the omitted content. While these longer letters may demand greater focus,

---

[128] Letters excluded from this set do not mean they are any less valuable but merely signify the constraints of letter selection.

Introduction

they are well worth reading, for they demonstrate Dutton's keen perspicacity when counselling believers in their unique struggles. With these self-contained and briefer inclusions, readers can profit from a sequence of more succinct conversations, at times deeply personal and moving, and always instructive. This, of course, is not only precious counsel for people in Dutton's time but also in ours. As such, letters have been titled by the editor in order to enable readers to turn to particular letters of personal relevance.

Part II also puts on display the very qualities that have described this woman thus far—one readily sought, esteemed for her wisdom, and dedicated in tending to the spiritual lives of all kinds of believers. In essence, these private letters are an explicit demonstration of Parts I and III: Dutton is counseling others in their walk with God and fulfilling her duty of love by nurturing them with soul-reviving truths.

Finally, the letters in this collection have been carefully edited to provide a more accessible read. The original unrevised version includes lengthy paragraphs; periodic sentences (in which the main point appears at the end of a very long sentence); unfamiliar punctuation usage; peculiar spelling (in addition to the "f" letter frequently being used in place of the "s"); and seemingly random capitalization and italicization of words. Editorial changes thus involved addressing these areas yet striving to remain faithful to the author's original style and intended impact.[129] The hope is that this collection of letters presents an amended text that draws rather than deters contemporary readers. In a culture that increasingly prefers reading for instant gratification, reading through these letters will, indeed, demand greater concentration and perseverance; in this regard, perhaps Dutton's advice offers some encouragement:

---

[129] Note that Watson's transcription of Dutton's autobiography includes "the original spellings, except the so-called 'long s' (f) becomes a regular 's'" (see her preface). The editor of this collection has applied similar revisions to Watson's transcriptions as those described at the end of this introduction.

The Spirituality of Anne Dutton

Oh, my dear friend, the way to glory in all the appointed paths of duty is uphill. To be religious in truth and sincerity and unto any growth and maturity, we are called to striving, running, fighting, wrestling.[130]

It has been a worthwhile undertaking to bring these letters of Dutton into your hands, and I pray that they will feed your soul as they have mine.

Priscilla Wong
June 2023

---

[130] Dutton, *Letters on Spiritual Subjects*, 38, Letter XI, To Mr. F------o.

PART I
Walking with God

"Thus God and man are agreed and meet together in the sweetest amity in his crucified Son, and without this it would be impossible for them to walk together.

Provenance

This collection begins with key passages from Anne Dutton's *A Discourse upon Walking with God: In a Letter to a Friend*.[1] Printed in 1735, it was not only one of Dutton's earliest publications but also one of her first direct replies to a correspondent seeking counsel.[2] The inquiry was made by a "dear servant of Christ in the ministry," whom she addresses in the letter as a "Dear and Honoured Brother."

Walking with God was widely distributed at home and abroad. Leaders in the eighteenth-century Evangelical Revival responded affirmatively to the work. George Whitefield, after reading it, informed Dutton in a letter that her "book on *Walking with God* has been blessed to one Mr. B____, and others in South Carolina."[3] Another reader was perhaps John Wesley; an entry in his diary in December 1740 reveals that he had read a book by Dutton, and Watson surmises that it was likely this one.[4]

Dutton begins this letter by expressing her gladness to hear that the Lord has brought this brother in Christ to minister to the "poor people at [Northhampton[5]]" and that she hopes he becomes a "useful instrument for the good of his dear children."[6] Specifically, Dutton exhorts

---

[1] Anne Dutton, *A Discourse upon Walking with God: In a Letter to a Friend...* (London: Printed for the author and sold by E. Gardner, 1735).

[2] Michael D. Sciretti Jr., "'Feed My Lambs': The Spiritual Direction Ministry of Calvinistic British Baptist Anne Dutton During the Early Years of Evangelical Revival" (Ph.D. diss., Baylor University, 2009), 122.

[3] *The Works of the Reverend George Whitefield*, 6 vols (London: Edward and Charles Dilley, 1771–1772) 1:250; Whitefield's letter 267, qtd. in Watson, *Volume 2: Discourses, Poetry, Hymns, Memoir*, ix.

[4] Arthur Wallington, "Wesley and Anne Dutton," *Proceedings of the Wesley Historical Society* 11/2 (June 1917): 45, qtd. in Watson, *Volume 2: Discourses, Poetry, Hymns, Memoir*, ix.

[5] The gentleman Dutton is writing to is likely Rev. Charles Rodgers of Northhampton. Sciretti, "Feed my Lambs," 120.

[6] Dutton, *Walking with God*, 3.

him to "be not discouraged from abiding with them because of their low estate, remembering that the Lord Jesus is with you." The poor people's low estate was in reference to their being without a pastor, for she writes in the ensuing lines, "Christ puts the feeding of his sheep and lambs upon your love to him[7] (especially now they have no shepherd)."

She then addresses the gentleman's "main request"—which is to instruct him on "the first principles of the mystery of walking with God." Her autobiography reveals that she had initially intended her response to this friend to be short, "that the subject was much too great and glorious for such a poor little worm to say anything about it," but she eventually engaged herself in the work because she felt that her all-sufficient Lord had led her to do it: "So said the Lord unto me, 'Let him come now unto me; bring the case to me. Though thou hast no ability to answer the request that is sent thee, I am well able to do it.'"[8] Though Dutton feels unworthy to answer this gentleman's question, she faithfully fulfills her duty, and she is later humbled by its incredible outcome: "as my God that would not suffer me to be ashamed, I attempted the work. And through his good hand upon me, [I] was delightfully carried through it and enlarged in my answer, much beyond what I thought of. And while I was engaged in the work, the Lord gave me a heart-melting intimation that it should be useful to souls."[9] This enlarged answer ultimately resulted in the penning of 170 pages, and while the original manuscript addresses two additional questions

---

[7] John 21:15–16.
[8] Watson, *Autobiography*, 162–163.
[9] Watson, *Autobiography*, 163.

Part I: Walking with God

inquired by the gentleman,[10] only Dutton's central discussion is excerpted here.[11]

Sermonic in style and structure,[12] *Walking with God* shows Dutton's profound understanding of the contours of the Christian journey.

---

[10] After extensive treatment of the first question, Dutton moves on to the gentleman's second question: "Dear brother, I shall commit the whole of this my answer to your first request to him that can ordain strength and perfect praise out of the mouth of babes and sucklings (Ps. 8:9; Matt. 21:16) and next attempt the solution of your second, which was that I would give you a few hints from Joseph's blessing." Dutton, *Walking with God*, 133–158. Here, Dutton explains how Joseph is a type of Christ.

Finally, Dutton proceeds to address her dear brother's final request, "Dear brother, your last request, which is implicit, contained in these words [I shall be glad to hear how my Lord dealt with you] (I suppose you mean, how he brought me into some measure of gospel liberty). I shall now attempt to answer in general as briefly as I can, it being my duty to be always ready to give a reason of the hope that is in me, with meekness and fear (1 Pet. 3:15)." Dutton then shares her personal testimony of how she arrived at the assurance of her salvation and the source of her Christian freedom. Dutton, *Walking with God*, 158–159.

[11] As indicated in the Introduction of this book, a cross-section of Dutton's central discussion has been presented here; in word count, it represents almost a third of the entire letter.

[12] Sciretti, "Feed My Lambs," 128.

1
A Discourse upon Walking with God:
In a Letter to a Friend

Dear and Honoured Brother,

… As to the main request of your letter, I said days should speak, and multitude of years should teach that wisdom.[1] At least those that are of full age and have their senses exercised.[2] And not such a babe as I, who have need that one to teach me what be the first principles of the mystery of walking with God.[3] Though for the time indeed, I might have attained a far greater proficiency of knowledge therein. But alas! I am a child that cannot speak.[4] Look up to Christ therefore as your prophet; his Spirit will teach you and give you fellowship with the mystery.

I doubt not, my dear brother, but you know far more what it is to walk with God than unworthy I. I am ashamed and confounded, and 'tis my daily burden that I can walk no more with him: I find such sad interruptions of communion. Indeed I see a ravishing glory in it, which at times draws out my soul into earnest longings after it; and I call them unspeakably happy that are blessed with a steady course of walking with God; but I count not myself to have attained.[5] You have much mistaken thoughts of me, for I am less than the least of all saints[6] and not worthy to be counted among the happy number that are honoured to walk with God.

---

[1] Job 32:7.
[2] Hebrews 5:14.
[3] Hebrews 5:12.
[4] Jeremiah 1:6.
[5] Philippians 3:12.
[6] Ephesians 3:8.

But yet, through grace, I have been so favoured as to know something of what it means. And though I fear I shall darken counsel by words without knowledge,[7] yet since you have desired me to tell you in some particulars what it is to walk with God, take it (as he shall open a babe's mouth) in the following hints. And,

First, to walk with God doth necessarily suppose an agreement between God and the soul.

Secondly, a way in which both walk.

Thirdly, a *continued course* or series of steps taken in that way.

Fourthly, free communion or mutual fellowship.

And fifthly, a sameness of intention, design, or end. ...

An agreement between God and the soul

First then, to walk with God doth necessarily suppose an agreement between God and the soul.

For how can two walk together except they be agreed?[8] All men, since the fall, are not only strangers to God but haters of him that say unto God, "Depart from us; we desire not the knowledge of thy ways."[9] And God, on the other hand, as a righteous revenging judge for the breach of his holy law, appears against the sinner in the condemning sentence thereof, arrayed in all the terrors of his wrath[10] so that it is impossible that there should be any friendship or communion with each other as such. ...

And as the first man, under the guilt of a broken law, hated God and fled from him, so doth every son of Adam to this day. But God knows his own that he has loved with an everlasting love[11] and ordained to the highest union and communion with himself in Christ.[12] And when the appointed moment of calling-love comes on, he sends the Spirit down

---

[7] Job 38:2.
[8] Amos 3:3.
[9] Ephesians 2:12; Romans 5:10 and 1:30; Job 21:14.
[10] Romans 3:5; Galatians 3:10; Nahum 1:2.
[11] 2 Timothy 2:19; Jeremiah 31:3.
[12] Acts 13:48; John 17:23.

Part I: Walking with God

into their hearts in the virtue of Christ's redeeming blood[13] to quicken them when dead in sins,[14] to create them anew in Christ[15] every way conformable to the image of his Son, the glorious pattern in his eye[16] that so they might be capable of the highest communion and sweetest intercourse with God.

And when thus made alive, the Holy Spirit sets before the eye of the new creature the misery of a natural state[17] and also reveals the glorious remedy,[18] preaching peace by Jesus Christ.[19] And as the enmity was fundamentally slain by Christ's death on the Cross,[20] so now, by the power of the Holy Ghost, it's actually slain in the virtue of his death brought into the soul. For now, God, as the God of love and peace, opens his heart unto the soul and shows it how he has loved it before time,[21] yea, loved it when dead in sins.[22] And from that great love did give Christ to it and for it.[23] To stand in its room, wounding him for its transgressions, that by his stripes it might be healed.[24] And that now justice being fully satisfied, he abundantly pardons all its iniquity.[25]

And while God thus manifests his everlasting love to the soul, oh, how it's drawn with loving-kindness to love him again![26] Now it looks on him it has pierced—and mourns,[27] loves what God loves, and hates what he hates. God hath nothing against the soul but rests in his love and rejoiceth over it with singing.[28] The soul hath nothing against God (so far as reconciled) but delightfully cleaves to him as its all in all.[29]

---

[13] Galatians 4:6.
[14] Ephesians 2:1.
[15] Ephesians 2:10.
[16] Romans 8:29.
[17] Romans 7:9.
[18] Galatians 1:16.
[19] Acts 10:36.
[20] Ephesians 2:16.
[21] Jeremiah 31:3.
[22] Ephesians 2:4–5.
[23] John 3:16.
[24] Isaiah 53:5.
[25] Isaiah 42:21, 55:7.
[26] 1 John 4:19.
[27] Zechariah 12:10.
[28] Zephaniah 3:17.
[29] Psalm 73:25–26.

The Spirit reveals God's love as a Father, Christ's [love] as a husband, and his own love as an Indweller and Comforter, and sweetly calls it into the freest intercourse.

And the soul, drawn by these love-cords,[30] delightfully obeys, forsaking all other lovers.[31] And is filled with astonishing wonder at infinite condescension that such a hell-deserving wretch that might have been a companion of devils and damned spirits should be admitted into the high privilege of fellowship with God in his three glorious persons through the man Christ Jesus. Aye, high indeed, higher than what innocent Adam was acquainted with, yea in some sense higher and more glorious than is conferred on the angels in heaven, for in Christ Jesus we stand in a nearer relation to God than angels. And God communicates of himself to every creature answerable to the relation it stands in to him.

Oh, adorable grace! Lord, what is man, filthy abominable man, that thou shouldst be mindful of him? And the Son of Man that thou settest thine heart upon him?[32] Thus God and man are agreed and meet together in the sweetest amity in his crucified Son. And without this it would be impossible for them to walk together. ...

A way in which both walk

Secondly, to walk with God doth necessarily suppose a way in which both God and the soul walk, which may be considered either comprehensively[33] or distributively.[34]

First, comprehensively. And so Christ is the way:[35] God's way to us and our way to God, and also the way in which all our mutual fellowship is maintained. I before considered Christ as the great meeting-place where God and the soul are agreed. And now I would hint

---

[30] Hosea 11:4.
[31] Isaiah 26:13; Hosea 14:8.
[32] Psalm 8:4; Job 15:16, 7:17.
[33] "Comprehensively" refers to the way in which Christ's work on the Cross enables the Christian to fully enjoy the privileges of communion with God.
[34] As Dutton later explains, "distributively" refers to "all the lesser paths comprehended in Christ." that is, by faith, instituted worship, divine providence, and conversational-holiness.
[35] John 14:6.

something of his being the great walking-place where every step of their delightful solace in and with each other is taken. ...

First, in his person as Mediator. ... All the infinite perfections and persons of the divine being dwell in him. The Father, Son, and Spirit dwell in Christ; and not only dwell in him but also walk in him in all the paths of grace towards the chosen of God. Thus, the apostle [says], "If we walk in the light as he is in the light, we have fellowship one with another."[36] By light, or holiness in this text (as I conceive), we are first to understand Christ himself, the true light, as he elsewhere calls him.[37] God, says he, is in Christ, dwells in him, walks in him; and if we walk where he walks, we have fellowship one with another. ...

Here now in Christ the way, as the man God's fellow,[38] the high and lofty one that inhabits eternity,[39] God can maintain the freest converse with that low thing—man—a creature of yesterday,[40] the work of his hands, without debasing his infinite majesty, yea, to the honour of all his divine perfections; for in Christ, all the promises of God are yea and Amen to the glory of God by us. ...[41]

Secondly, he is also the way as our Kinsman-Redeemer that has obtained eternal redemption for us.[42]

And as such he is the great medium of converse between God and sinners. ... He not only voluntarily undertook to pay the vast sums we owed from whence it became a righteous thing with God to demand satisfaction at his hands, but he also in the fullness of time (according to his engagement from everlasting) assumed our nature,[43] sustained our persons,[44] fulfilled the law for us,[45] [bore][46] our sins,[47] was made a

---

[36] John 1:7.
[37] John 1:9.
[38] Zechariah 13:7.
[39] Isaiah 57:15.
[40] Job 8:9.
[41] 2 Corinthians 1:20.
[42] Hebrews 9:12.
[43] Hebrews 2:16.
[44] Colossians 1:18.
[45] Matthew 5:17 with Romans 5:18.
[46] Altered from *bare* (archaic).
[47] 1 Peter 2:24.

curse,[48] conflicted with the powers of darkness,[49] endured his Father's wrath,[50] and at last died in our room,[51] descended into the grave,[52] and rose again for our justification.[53] And having finished his work below, he ascended to glory in the triumphs of his conquest,[54] attended with the chariots of God and the shout of thousands of angels, as the Lord strong and mighty, the Lord mighty in battle.[55] And as our great representing-head, he entered into the holiest of all and sat down at the right hand of the majesty on high.[56] And by this discharge of his suretiship[57] engagements, he has answered all the [laws'] demands,[58] satisfied justice,[59] made an end of sin,[60] spoiled principalities and powers,[61] established a lasting peace between God and us,[62] made reconciliation for iniquity and brought in an everlasting righteousness, yea, has brought us in it in his own person into the presence of his and our Father,[63] presenting us in the body of his flesh, through death holy and unblameable and unreproveable in his sight.[64] Thus Christ is the way in what he is to us and has done for us in which God walks with his poor sinful children.

Here all the divine perfections harmonize. Mercy and truth meet together; righteousness and peace kiss each other.[65] Here it is that God

---

[48] Galatians 3:13.
[49] Luke 22:53.
[50] Matthew 27:46.
[51] Romans 5:6.
[52] Ephesians 4:9.
[53] Romans 4:25.
[54] Ephesians 4:10.
[55] Psalm 68:17–18; with 47:5 and 24:8.
[56] Hebrews 9:24; 1:3.
[57] Meaning, "The office of a surety or bondsman; the act of being bound for another." Johnson, Samuel. "Suretiship." *A Dictionary of the English Language*, https://johnsonsdictionaryonline.com/1755/suretiship_ns, 1755. Accessed May 27, 2023.
[58] Romans 10:4.
[59] Isaiah 42:21.
[60] Daniel 9:24.
[61] Colossians 2:15.
[62] Colossians 1:20.
[63] John 20:17.
[64] Colossians 1:22.
[65] Psalms 85:10.

Part I: Walking with God

can be just and yet the justifier of him that believes in Jesus.[66] Just to forgive us our sins and to cleanse us from all unrighteousness.[67] Just in abundant pardon, multiplying to pardon the multiplied sins of our daily provocations.[68] And it was the glorious display of this grace, in his walk with us in Christ, [that] made the prophet break forth as being filled with astonishing wonder: "Who is a God like unto thee, that pardoneth iniquity, and passeth by the transgression of the remnant of his heritage? He retaineth not his anger forever, because he delighteth in mercy."[69]

Here's room for God to walk with us in his everlasting kindness,[70] covenant-faithfulness,[71] abundant goodness,[72] infinite wisdom, ordering all things for our good.[73] And in his almighty power sustaining us under our weakness, defending us from our enemies by which we are kept as in a garrison through faith unto salvation.[74]

Again, here's room also for us to walk with God in all relations, with suitable dispositions. With God as a Father;[75] Christ as a husband, brother, friend;[76] with the Holy Ghost as an indweller, sanctifier, and comforter:[77] For the blood of Jesus cleanseth us from all sin[78] and gives us boldness in the presence of God.[79] His righteousness clothes us;[80] his fullness supplies us;[81] his merits present us and all our services acceptable to God. ...[82]

---

[66] Romans 3:26.
[67] 1 John 1:9.
[68] Isaiah 55:7.
[69] Micah 7:18.
[70] Isaiah 54:8.
[71] Psalm 80:33.
[72] Jeremiah 31:14.
[73] Ephesians 1:8; Romans 8:28.
[74] 1 Peter 1:5.
[75] Ephesians 5:1.
[76] Psalm 45:11; Hebrews 2:11; John 15:14.
[77] Ephesians 4:30.
[78] 1 John 1:7.
[79] Hebrews 10:19.
[80] Isaiah 61:10.
[81] John 1:16.
[82] 1 Peter 2:5.

Secondly, the way may also be considered distributively. And thus all the lesser paths comprehended in Christ the great way may be so styled. And the way in this respect may be reduced to four general heads:

First, the way of faith.
Secondly, the way of instituted worship.
Thirdly, the way of divine providence.
And fourthly, the way of conversation-holiness.

The way of faith

First, the way of faith. By which I intend the doctrine of faith or the way of divine revelation called the way of God[83] in which God walks with his own in peculiar grace, revealing to these babes the mysteries of the gospel while they are hid from the wise and prudent world.[84] The divine revelation is alike made to all in the written Word; but God makes it a way in which he manifests himself unto us so as he doth not unto the world.[85] Our eyes have the blessedness to see[86] while they seeing see not. ...[87]

And as in this way of faith doctrinally, divine revelation, God walks with his in the sovereignty of his grace, so they also, herein, walk with him in the obedience of faith practically.[88] The grace of faith as a fruit of the Spirit in the souls of believers[89] is a principle suited to the doctrine of faith. As an eye, it looks to faith's object;[90] as a hand, it lays hold thereon;[91] and as a foot, it walks therein.[92] While all the glorious doctrines of faith, shining in Christ the path of the just[93] by the Holy Ghost's light, become as so many high places on which the soul

---

[83] Acts 18:26.
[84] Matthew 11:25; 1 Corinthians 2:10.
[85] John 14:22.
[86] Matthew 13:16.
[87] Matthew 13:13.
[88] Romans 16:26.
[89] Galatians 5:22.
[90] Hebrews 12:2.
[91] Hebrews 6:18.
[92] Colossians 2:6.
[93] Proverbs 4:18.

delightfully walks with God.[94] In this way of faith, all the famous worthies mentioned in the eleventh of the Hebrews walked with God; yea, all the saints that ever were, are, or shall be, have, do, and shall walk here.

And further, God calls all his children (though some in a more eminent manner than others) to walk with him in this way of faith, even when they want the light of spiritual sense. God always walks with his in Christ according to the revelation of his mind to them, though not always apparently. And they answerably walk with him in faith, receiving his divine testimony, setting to their seal that he is true,[95] judging him both able and faithful who hath promised,[96] and as such trusting in him even when he seems to slay them.[97] When dark dispensations cover them and they have no light of sense to walk by, yet even then can they trust in the Lord and stay themselves upon their God. ...[98]

The way of instituted worship
Secondly, instituted worship is another way in which God and his people walk with each other. ... The moral obligation whereto we have in the first command, "Thou shalt have no other God but me,"[99] "Thou shalt worship the Lord thy God and him only shalt thou serve."[100] The particular direction whereof is contained in the Scriptures of the Old and New Testament.[101] God in Old Testament times made revelation of his mind herein to his people by his holy prophets and eminently by that great prophet Moses, but in these last days of New Testament times, he hath spoke unto us by his Son.[102] According as Moses had long ago foretold, "A prophet shall the Lord your God raise up unto

---

[94] Habakkuk 3:19.
[95] John 3:33.
[96] Romans 4:21; Hebrews 11:11.
[97] Job 13:15.
[98] Isaiah 50:10.
[99] Exodus 20:3.
[100] Matthew 4:10.
[101] 2 Timothy 3:16-17.
[102] Hebrews 1:2.

you like unto me; unto him shall ye hearken."[103] Christ as the great prophet of the church, the Son over his own house[104] hath made a complete revelation of the divine will relating to gospel-worship, which the faith of New Testament saints delightfully submits to, owning Christ as prophet, and also as king in Zion....

Further, as the churches are built together for a habitation of God through the Spirit,[105] so he also walks there: "I will walk in them," says God,[106] which, if true of particular believers, is much more so of the churches....

Oh, infinite condescension! Will God indeed dwell with men on earth![107] Will the high and lofty one, the great I AM,[108] familiarly walk with worms that are less than nothing and vanity![109] Will he that is far above all blessing and praise,[110] that humbleth himself to behold the worship of heaven,[111] yet bow down a gracious ear to the chattering prayers and praises of mortal, sinful men whose foundation is in the dust![112] 'Tis well for us that this path of divine worship is comprehended in Christ, else God and we could never walk together in it.

The way of divine providence
But thirdly, divine providence is also a way in which God and his people walk together, which may be divided into two parts, prosperous and afflictive.

First, *prosperous:* The saints are indeed for the most part a poor and an afflicted people,[113] but yet some prosperity, more or less, our dear Father is pleased to afford to all his children. They are heirs of

---

[103] Deuteronomy 18:15.
[104] Hebrews 3:6.
[105] Ephesians 2:22.
[106] 2 Corinthians 6:16.
[107] 2 Chronicles 6:18.
[108] Isaiah 57:15; Exodus 3:14.
[109] Isaiah 40:17.
[110] Nehemiah 9:5.
[111] Psalm 113:6.
[112] Psalm 31:2; Isaiah 38:14; Job 4:19.
[113] Zephaniah 3:12.

promise,[114] and godliness hath the promise of the life that now is as well as that which is to come.[115] All things are theirs and the world among the rest.[116] They are heirs of it.[117] The meek shall inherit the earth.[118] And they are entered upon the possession of it now by faith, in that measure of it infinite wisdom has allotted for every child. ...

And the wicked, generally speaking, have the greatest share of outward good things, their portion being in this life.[119] But God walks with his own in a very distinguishing manner from the world in the way of providential bounty. They are blessed in their basket and store, in their coming in and going out, and in all they set their hand unto.[120] Aye, blessed indeed, for in blessing they are blessed.[121] They have the inside of the blessing (God's heart in every favour they enjoy) while others have only the outside; nay, their very blessings are cursed to them.[122] And the prosperity of fools destroys them.[123] Hence it is, "A little that a righteous man hath is better than the riches of many wicked."[124] The saints see the fountain whence all their blessings flow[125] while others boast of their wealth as if gotten by their own hand.[126] They possess all things as their own in Christ,[127] while the wicked, alas! have no spiritual right to the least bit or drop.[128] They see the face of God in every smile of providence,[129] but if favour be shown to the wicked, they behold not

---

[114] Hebrews 6:17.
[115] 1 Timothy 4:8.
[116] 1 Corinthians 3:21–22.
[117] Romans 4:13.
[118] Matthew 5:5.
[119] Psalm 17:14.
[120] Deuteronomy 28:5–6, etc.
[121] Genesis 22:17.
[122] Malachi 2:2.
[123] Proverbs 1:32.
[124] Psalm 37:16.
[125] 1 Chronicles 29:14.
[126] Psalm 49:6.
[127] 2 Corinthians 6:10.
[128] Proverbs 16:8.
[129] Genesis 33:10.

the majesty of the Lord.[130] God's people taste and see that the Lord is good in every mercy. ...[131]

And oh, the glory of God's walk with his in his wonder-working providence![132] ... And as God walks with his in the bounties of his providence as their own God and Father,[133] supplying all their need,[134] so they also herein walk with him as his dear children,[135] not trusting in uncertain riches but in the living God who gives them all things richly to enjoy,[136] honouring the Lord with their substance.[137] And in everything giving thanks to the glory of his great name.[138]

... Secondly, afflictive providence is a way in which God and his people walk together. ... God hath his way in which he walks in mercy with his own, even in affliction-storms.[139] Through much tribulation they must enter the kingdom.[140] They are predestinated to be conformable unto Christ in sufferings as well as in glory.[141] But himself having born their sorrows and carried their griefs,[142] the curse is taken out of them, and it's given unto them on the behalf of Christ, not only to believe but also to suffer for his sake.[143] They fill up but what is behind of the afflictions of Christ in their flesh.[144] And when they pass through the waters, the Lord being with them, the rivers don't overflow them, and through the fires, the flame doth not kindle upon them.[145]

---

[130] Isaiah 26:10.
[131] Psalm 34:8.
[132] Psalm 107:8.
[133] Psalm 67:6; 103:13.
[134] Philippians 4:9.
[135] Ephesians 5:1.
[136] 1 Timothy 6:17.
[137] Proverbs 3:9.
[138] 1 Thessalonians 5:18; 1 Corinthians 10:30–31.
[139] Nahum 1:3, with Psalm 25:10.
[140] Acts 14:22.
[141] Romans 8:29, 17.
[142] Isaiah 53:4.
[143] Philippians 1:29.
[144] Colossians 1:24.
[145] Isaiah 43:2.

Part I: Walking with God

In this way of afflictive providence, God walks with his people in covenant-faithfulness[146] as a wise, tender, gracious Father,[147] working all things after the counsel of his own will for the good of his children[148] and the glory of his own name.[149] He rebukes them in love;[150] chastens them for their profit that they might be partakers of his holiness;[151] blesseth his chastening hand; and teacheth them out of his law,[152] opening their ear and sealing their instruction.[153] By these he purgeth out their corruptions,[154] trieth their graces,[155] and prepares them for an eternal weight of glory.[156]

God's people also walk with him herein (so far as his love is shed abroad in their hearts) by submitting to his divine sovereignty,[157] putting their mouths in the dust,[158] justifying him in all his proceedings,[159] acknowledging his infinite goodness,[160] and glorifying him in the fire.[161] Here they learn to keep God's commandments,[162] humble themselves under his mighty hand,[163] [and] are patient in tribulation.[164] Yea, rejoice and glory in it also,[165] knowing that when in the furnace of affliction,[166] the Lord sits by as a refiner,[167] and that when he has tried them, they shall come forth as gold.[168] Aye, not only doth the Lord sit by when they

---

[146] Psalm 89:30, etc.; 119:75.
[147] Romans 11:33; Psalm 103:13.
[148] Ephesians 1:11; Romans 8:28.
[149] John 11:4.
[150] Revelation 3:19.
[151] Hebrews 12:10.
[152] Psalm 94:12.
[153] Job 33:16.
[154] Isaiah 27:9.
[155] 1 Peter 1:6–7; Romans 5:3–4.
[156] 2 Corinthians 4:17.
[157] Psalm 39:9.
[158] Lamentations 3:29.
[159] Matthew 11:19.
[160] Ezra 9:13.
[161] Isaiah 24:15.
[162] Psalm 119:67.
[163] James 4:10.
[164] Romans 12:12.
[165] 2 Corinthians 7:4; Romans 5:3.
[166] Isaiah 43:10.
[167] Malachi 3:3.
[168] Job 23:10.

are in fiery trials but is with them there, which will make them walk at liberty in the midst of a burning fiery furnace. ....[169]

And what an eminent instance hereof was holy Job? The Lord sends one affliction upon the neck of another, takes away his substance, bereaves him of his children, strips him quite naked. But how doth Job take this? Will he flee off now and walk no more with God? No, no. He can give God leave to do what he will, with him or his, and not be angry. He falls down and worships, acknowledgeth infinite goodness, adores divine sovereignty, and blesseth the name of Jehovah for taking as well as giving. "Then Job arose, and rent his mantle, and shaved his head, and fell down upon the ground and worshipped. Naked came I out of my mother's womb, and naked shall I return thither: the Lord gave, and the Lord hath taken away, and blessed be the name of the Lord."

But the time would fail me to multiply instances recorded in God's book. Thus, all the prophets and Old Testament saints walked with God in afflictions. And here the apostles and New Testament saints walked also in a glorious advance of gospel light and liberty. Aye, here they walk with God, not only in afflictions, but in afflictions unto death if God calls them to it. They count not their lives dear that they may finish their course with joy[170] but pass on triumphing through all difficulties, tribulation, distress, persecution, famine, nakedness, peril, or sword as more than conquerors through him that hath loved them.[171]

Oh, this walking with God in tribulation! It's a joy the stranger intermeddles not with.[172] But thus all the saints, according to their several degrees of faith and light, do more or less walk with God in this way of afflictive providence. And as God walks with his herein—to sympathize with them in all their sorrows,[173] to sustain them under all their burdens,[174] and to do them good by every stroke[175]—so also in his own time

---

[169] Daniel 3:25.
[170] Acts 20:24.
[171] Romans 8:35, 37.
[172] Proverbs 14:10.
[173] Isaiah 63:9.
[174] Psalm 55:22.
[175] Psalm 119:71.

completely and gloriously to deliver them,[176] which they by faith trust the Lord for,[177] nor doth he disappoint their expectation.[178]

The Lord will not contend forever.[179] His fatherly anger in providential frowns endureth but for a moment; weeping may endure while the night of affliction lasteth; but joy cometh in morning of deliverance, for in his favour there is life.[180] He doth not willingly afflict his children.[181] 'Tis but if need be they are in heaviness.[182] And when he speaks against them, and they are in the midst of distresses, he earnestly remembers them still, and his bowels are troubled for them.[183] But to exercise loving-kindness, he therein delighteth.[184] Judgment is his strange act,[185] but to walk with his people in the pure unmixed displays of his goodness is his native delight. When he thus does them good, it's with his whole heart and his whole soul.[186] And as God walks with his people in all his providential ways, which are mercy and truth,[187] whether prosperous or afflictive, so they answerably walk with him herein in duty and thankfulness. And O happy souls that are honoured to walk with God in all the providential changes that pass over them!

The way of conversation-holiness
Fourthly, conversation-holiness is another way in which God and his people walk together, called the way of God's commandments …

Herein the saints are commanded to walk: "But as he that hath called you is holy, so be ye holy in all manner of conversation."[188] And it may be distinguished from heart-holiness or the new nature in the souls of the saints communicated out of Christ's fullness by the Holy

---

[176] Psalm 34:19.
[177] Psalm 22:8.
[178] Psalm 9:18.
[179] Isaiah 57:16.
[180] Psalm 30:5.
[181] Lamentations 3:33.
[182] 1 Peter 1:6.
[183] Jeremiah 31:20.
[184] Jeremiah 9:24.
[185] Isaiah 28:21.
[186] Jeremiah 32:41.
[187] Psalm 25:10.
[188] 1 Peter 1:15.

Spirit, this being the principle from whence it proceeds. All holy actions must have a holy principle from whence they flow, a holy rule to which they are conformed, and a holy end to which they are directed. Love to God is the principle, his Word the rule, and his glory the end. Conversation-holiness extends itself to thoughts, words, and actions. Holy thoughts are the walk of a holy soul with God immediately; holy words and actions, so far as before men, its walk with him remotely.

And that God and the soul sweetly walk together in this way of holiness is plain: God is light, and in him is no darkness at all. If we walk in the light as he is in the light, we have fellowship one with another....[189] And generally speaking, those that walk most holily are most favoured with God's sensible presence.

In this way of conversation-holiness God walks with his people:

First, by teaching them his statutes, which the Psalmist so often prays for.[190]

Secondly, by heart-attracting, soul-transforming discoveries of the glory of his holiness and the excellency of all his righteous precepts.

And thirdly, by free and full acceptation of all their holy performances.

In the first, he walks with us as the Lord our God that teacheth us to profit, leading us in the way where we should go.[191]

In the second, he sets his own holiness before us as a pattern and gives us to see the excellency of all his holy ways to raise and ennoble our spirits: "Be ye holy, for I am holy";[192] perfect, as your Father is perfect.[193]

And in the third, he walks with us as a tender, gracious father, pitying all our weakness, pardoning all our sinfulness, and continually accepting all our services with the highest complacency and well-pleasedness.[194] And the saints answerably walk with God herein. ...

---

[189] 1 John 1:5, 7.
[190] Psalm 119.
[191] Isaiah 48:17.
[192] 1 Peter 1:16.
[193] Matthew 5:48.
[194] 1 Peter 2:5.

Part I: Walking with God

Further, this conversation-holiness extends itself unto a walking with God in every place, station, relation, and circumstances of life, whether spiritual, natural, or civil; in the church, family, or commonwealth. Hence, every man is exhorted, in that calling wherein he is called, therein to abide with God.[195]… And O! With what unspeakable pleasure doth a holy soul walk with God in all relative duties, rejoicing that the Lord hath commanded them, that so it may perform them under that very notion of obedience.[196] There's not a common action of life, but it would interest God in.[197]

Oh, how easy is Christ's yoke and how light his burden to the saints walking with God under the sweet constraints of his love.[198] Wisdom's ways are to them pleasantness, and all her paths are peace.[199] They're not their own.[200] And whether they live, they live unto the Lord; and whether they die, they die unto the Lord. Living and dying, they are the Lord's.[201] They count all that part of their life lost in which they do not live unto God, all their time lost that is not spent for his glory. Yea, there is such a holy eagerness in their souls after walking with God that makes them count all their former walk with him not worth the name. There is still set before them such an intensive, extensive, and perpetual way of walking with God in holiness, which their feet have yet never traced that makes them forget the things that are behind and reach forth after those which are before; and the more holiness any soul attains, the more eager it is in its pursuit after it.

A continued series of steps taken in that way

Thirdly, a *continued course* or series of steps taken therein. God not only begins to walk with us in Christ, but he goes on with us in him as our everlasting friend. …

---

[195] 1 Corinthians 7:24.
[196] Psalm 119:111.
[197] 1 Corinthians 10:31.
[198] Matthew 11:30; 2 Corinthians 5:14.
[199] Proverbs 3:17.
[200] 1 Corinthians 6:19.
[201] Romans 14:8.

Time makes no alteration in his heart, no, nor his people's sins neither. Not all our lowness, baseness, vileness, and daily provocations can wean his heart from us. He has chosen such foolish, base, vile, provoking worms as we to be his everlasting companions.[202] He hath desired to walk with us[203]— us—not our vileness, yet it's us, not withstanding our vileness. O amazing grace! …

In this mystery then of God's walking with us and we with him, we are to observe a *continued course.* God not only begins to walk with us at first in the person of Christ as the alone Mediator and in him also as the great Redeemer, but he continues to go on with us in this great way according to his unchangeable heart-love,[204] the unchangeable dignity of the Mediator's person,[205] and the eternal efficacy of the Redeemer's merits.[206] Christ as our great high-priest not only made peace for us on the Cross, but he also maintains it for us on the throne. He was once dead but is alive and lives for evermore[207] to maintain an everlasting friendship between God and us.

We are poor sinful, sinning creatures, and Satan our grand Enemy is always accusing us day and night before God.[208] But Christ always appears in the presence of God for us[209] as our righteous advocate to plead our cause.[210] If Satan accuse us, Christ pleads what he is to us and has done for us to the full satisfaction of law and justice, and so he brings us off clear in a way of righteousness with honour in open court. If Satan improve the charges he brings against us to show how unworthy we are that God should continue to walk with us, Christ pleads his own worthiness and the interest he hath in his Father's heart as also the inseparable relation and union grace has taken us into, which always prevails with the Father for continued communion.…

---

[202] 1 Corinthians 1:27–28; Job 40:4; Isaiah 62:5.
[203] Psalm 132:13.
[204] Jeremiah 31:3; Malachi 3:6.
[205] Romans 9:5; Hebrews 13:8.
[206] Hebrews 9:12; 10:14.
[207] Revelation 1:18.
[208] Revelation 12:10.
[209] Hebrews 9:24.
[210] 1 John 2:1.

Part I: Walking with God

But if any man sin (let him not sink under it and be discouraged as if the God of all grace would break friendship and walk no more with him), for we have an advocate with the Father, Jesus Christ, the Righteous, that lives in heaven on purpose to maintain fellowship between God and us. And because he lives, we shall live also.[211] Thus the apostle to the Romans, "If, when we were enemies, we were reconciled to God by the death of his Son, much more, being reconciled, we shall be saved by his life."[212]

… And oh, blessed be God, grace is a boundless ocean that all the multiplied streams can never draw dry. It has been streaming forth continually in all its various channels to all the saints in all the ages of time, and yet there is never the less in it. The God of all grace has as much grace in his heart to walk with us now in these latter ages of the world as he had when he first began to walk with Adam, Enoch, Noah, etc. …

But then we must observe that the Lord always walks with us really for our advantage, yet not always sensibly to our perception. Christ walked with the disciples going to Emmaus, and they felt glorious effects of his presence; but yet their eyes were holden that they knew him not.[213] And thus it is oft-times with God's dear children: for though as the mountains are round about Jerusalem, so the Lord is round about his people from henceforth and forever.[214] Yet they, poor hearts, oft think he is far from them, as the church [laments],[215] "Mine eye runneth down with water, because the comforter [that] should relieve my soul is far from me." And yet the comforter ever abides with us,[216] though his comforting influences are at times suspended.[217]

And thus our God continually walks with us, though at times he covers himself with such thick darkness that veils the glory of his face from our sight.[218] Faith, indeed, can pierce the cloud and see him

---

[211] John 14:19.
[212] Romans 5:10.
[213] Luke 24:13–16.
[214] Psalm 125:2.
[215] Lamentations 1:16.
[216] John 14:16.
[217] Psalm 51:12.
[218] Psalm 97:2.

continually with us, holding us by his right hand that we shall not be moved.[219] But alas! It's oft impenetrable to spiritual sense. ...

But, oh how a fresh discovery of this grace makes a weary child of God just ready to faint under absence and want of sensible influences to renew its strength, to mount up with wings as eagles, to run and not be weary, to walk and not faint![220] God's continual walking with us is our safety, the faith of it our comfort. ...

God's continual walk with his people is managed in such a depth and variety of infinite wisdom that his judgments are oft to us unsearchable, and his ways herein past finding out.[221] And when the glory of his constant walk with us is obscured from our sight, 'tis but a preparation for the brighter display of his everlasting kindness herein; when like the sun from under an eclipse, he breaks out upon us again with a new amazing glory, which is exceedingly pleasant for our eyes to behold. ...[222]

And though deadness and inactivity oft seize their spirits, yet Christ is such a living way that communicates life to them every step they take in him. In this way of righteousness is life and in the pathway thereof, there is no death.[223] And though as to their continual walking in this way, there arise many obstacles from their own sinfulness and unworthiness, yet it being a way prepared on purpose for them in these respects,[224] the Lord takes up the stumbling blocks and makes their way plain before them so that they pass on safely.

Yea, he makes the vision of life and love so plain in this way that they run and read it with unspeakable pleasure.[225] When God revealed Christ at first to the souls of his children as their only way of walking with him, he was, as such, exceeding precious to their faith[226] in all his

---

[219] Psalm 73:23.
[220] Isaiah 40:30.
[221] Romans 11:33.
[222] Ecclesiastes 11:7.
[223] Proverbs 12:28.
[224] 1 Timothy 1:15; Romans 4:16.
[225] Isaiah 57:14; Proverbs 15:19; Psalm 78:53; Habakkuk 2:2.
[226] 1 Peter 2:7.

suitable fullness to their various wants;[227] and as they received him, so they continually walk in him in every step they take with God, even to their dying moments. Glad were they at first as poor, nothing, filthy, guilty creatures to run into this name of the Lord as their high, holy, righteous way where only they might walk with God and be safe.[228]

And they are still of the same mind. Christ has lost no glory in their eye. They think they need him as much as ever. Yea, some of the saints, the further they advance, think they need him more than ever. For though as they pass on in Christ, their personal holiness increaseth, yet the more holy they are, the more humble. Because the Holy Ghost, in managing this work upon their souls, discovers still greater and greater abominations in their hearts:[229] on the one hand, to keep them low in their own eyes, as on the other, he opens transcendent views of the glory of Christ to keep him high in their esteem.

Hence it is that they dare not take a step with God in any other way but Christ, whatever temptations they have thereto. If Satan present a pleasing prospect of their own obedience, and their unbelieving hearts cast an adulterous glance upon it, this, under the Holy Ghost's convincing work,[230] makes them loath themselves so much the more in their own sight,[231] esteeming themselves but as an unclean thing, and their best righteousness but as filthy rags,[232] yea, as loss and dung, in comparison of the knowledge of Christ as their only way to walk with God. Oh! 'tis in him they would be found.[233] For as the Holy Ghost's voice exalts Christ alone in the soul,[234] so the voice of the new creature doth as it were echo back the sound: none but Christ, none but Christ, Christ is all in all.[235] We are, saith the apostle, of the circumcision that worship God in Spirit, that rejoice in Christ Jesus (in him only, in him always)

---

[227] Colossians 1:19.
[228] Proverbs 18:10.
[229] Ezekiel 8:6.
[230] Job 16:9.
[231] Ezekiel 20:43.
[232] Isaiah 64:6.
[233] Philippians 3:8–9.
[234] John 16:14.
[235] Colossians 3:11.

and have no confidence in the flesh.[236] The holiest saint on earth dares not set up his own personal holiness abstracted from Christ as a way to walk with God in. No, they see such imperfections therein, they dare not. Yea, they see such a transcendent excellency in Christ that though they were perfect, they would not know their soul. They would despise their life.[237] And as they go on continually to walk with God in Christ their great way, so in all the lesser paths comprehended in him. …

Objection: It may be objected, "How can such sinful creatures as we be said continually to walk with God in all these respects?"

Answer: To which I answer that though the term [walking] doth imply a *continued course,* yet when applied to our walking with God, it is not to be understood strictly as if there were no interruptions in it, though it may and ought to be understood as denoting a *general course.*

Thus, Asa's heart is said to be perfect all his days.[238] And though in the latter end of his life he grievously sinned, for in his affliction he sought not to the Lord but to the physicians,[239] yet because his heart was perfect in his *general course,* he is said to be perfect all his days. …

Thus, there are sad interruptions in the saints' walk with God, and yet in regard of their *general course,* they may be said so to do, there being no place, relation, or station of life in which they do not more or less walk with him.

Yea, according to the mind of the inner man, there is no circumstance in which they do not begin, go on, and end it with God. Their walk with God is perfect in respect of parts in that they walk with him in all the parts of obedience, both as to faith and practice, having respect unto all his commandments.[240] But yet, even in the greatest saint, it falls far short in respect of degrees. And if God was to mark iniquity, the holiest man upon earth could not stand before him as a walker with

---

[236] Philippians 3:3.
[237] Job 9:21.
[238] 2 Chronicles 15:17.
[239] 2 Chronicles 16:12.
[240] Psalm 119:6.

him.[241] But oh! Blessed be his name, there is forgiveness with him, that he may be feared.[242]

And while we have fellowship one with another, the blood of Jesus Christ his Son cleanseth us from all sin.[243] As dear children, we walk with God as a Father who, in infinite grace and boundless compassion, pities our weakness, pardons our shortness, and kindly accepts the desires of our souls to walk with him, calling that walking (which we think not worth the name and is indeed rather staggering and feeble) attempting than walking.

Oh, amazing grace! Christ will say to the righteous, I was hungry, and ye fed me; naked, and ye clothed me. But what will be their answer? Amazed at his grace in owning their weak services, they'll say, Lord, when did we do this or that unto thee? We never did anything for thee worthy of thy notice.[244] Thus in respect of God's gracious acceptance of their *general course*, all the saints may be said to walk with God....

Little children, young men, fathers[245]

And as there are to be found among the saints very different degrees in their walking with God as it respects different persons, so respecting the same soul at different times.

Some of the saints walk as little children who, though fond of their Father's company, yet being weak, are but slow in their pace and often fall. Some as young men, arrived to a full age, are nimble in their course, being strong in faith and in the grace that is in Christ Jesus to surmount all the difficulties they meet with in their way. And others there are that walk with God in the solid wisdom of fathers. ...

At first, the soul begins to walk with God in abundance of holy fondness, though with a great deal of weakness, which the Lord takes

---

[241] Psalm 130:3.
[242] Psalm 130:4.
[243] 1 John 1:7.
[244] Matthew 25:35, 37.
[245] Editor's subtitle

exceeding kindly: "I remember thee," says he, "the kindness of thy youth, when thou wentest after me in a wilderness."[246]

But as it grows up in Christ to the state of manhood, it walks stronger and further with God. It can run greater lengths with him than at first, for it goes from strength to strength.[247]

At first, if it did not see its Father's smiles, it could not walk with him in the faith of his love. But now, though he should hide himself and appear against it as an enemy, yet it will trust in him though he should slay it.[248] And it continues to walk with him in the faith of his love when there are nothing but frowns upon his face....

God loves his children, and he exceedingly delights in being loved by them again. Intense love finds its greatest pleasure in being ardently loved by the beloved object. And for creatures of the same make thus to seek for and find a mutual love-complacency in each other is no strange thing.

But that God, the glorious God, the great I AM who is self-sufficient to his own happiness and needs none of his creatures to make any addition thereto, should yet, nevertheless, set his heart upon such worthless, sinful worms as we and not only give us leave to love him but count himself happy in our love—[249]may well fill heaven and earth with wonder! Lord, "What is man, that thou art thus mindful of him?"[250] is a theme fitted to the astonishing wonder of men and angels. ...[251]

But oh! How this wonderful grace melts the soul, humbles it under all its backslidings, and quickens it to walk with God in all the paths of obedience!... But when the soul again is made sensible of its decays in love—oh, how it's ashamed and confounded in the remembrance of all its wandering ways![252] And sometimes it don't know whether it walks with God at all. It looks upon its defiled feet[253] and is ready to faint away

---

[246] Jeremiah 2:2.
[247] Psalm 84:7.
[248] Job 13:15.
[249] Isaiah 62:5.
[250] Psalm 8:4.
[251] 1 Peter 1:12.
[252] Ezekiel 16:61.
[253] John 13:10; Luke 5:8.

Part I: Walking with God

in self-loathing. But then the everlasting love of God is its cordial[254] and the meritorious blood of Christ its bath, and so again, it goes up from the washing clean and strong.[255] Thus it walks with God while a young man until it arrives to the state of fatherhood.

And then it walks with him in the solid and extensive wisdom of a father, being well-acquainted with all manner of ways of walking with God. The excellency of its walk when a child lies in its love: to aim at a great deal when it can do little; when a young man, in its strength: to overcome opposition; and when a father, in its wisdom: to walk with God steadily and comprehensively. "When I was a child," says the apostle, "I spoke as a child, I understood as a child, I thought as a child: but when I became a man, I put away childish things."[256]

But yet, alas! In the best of saints there is such imperfection in their walk with God that we may well wonder he'll give it the name. The grace that shines forth herein is amazing to us now and will be matter of astonishment in the day of Christ when he'll open it before men and angels, saying, "Come, ye blessed of my Father, inherit the kingdom prepared for you from the foundation of the world...." ...The Lord delights in the walk of his children now,[257] their feet being "shod with the preparation of the gospel of peace."[258] Yea, he admires it, "How beautiful are thy feet with shoes, O prince's daughter!"[259] And he'll openly show his grace in commending it ere long, for all our walk by faith in this world[260] will be found unto praise, honour, and glory in the world to come.

---

[254] Meaning, "1. A medicine that increases the force of the heart, or quickens the circulation. 2. Any medicine that increases strength. 3. Any thing that comforts, gladdens, and exhilarates." Johnson, Samuel. "cordial." *A Dictionary of the English Language*, https://johnsonsdictionaryonline.com/views/search.php?term=cordial, 1755. Accessed June 18, 2023.

[255] Song of Solomon 6:6.

[256] 1 Corinthians 13:11.

[257] Psalm 37:23.

[258] Ephesians 6:15.

[259] Song of Songs 7:1.

[260] 2 Corinthians 5:7.

The Spirituality of Anne Dutton

Communion and fellowship

Fourthly, free communion and mutual fellowship. Communion and fellowship, which as I intend it here, consists in a free opening of hearts and a mutual delight in each other's company as is oft found in persons walking together in agreement. Thus, of good men it is said, "He that walketh with wise men shall be wise."[261]

... And since God and his people walk together in the most perfect agreement as friends,[262] and in the sweetest relations as father and children,[263] as bridegroom and bride,[264] as comforter and comforted,[265] their communion must needs be exceeding sweet, and their mutual love-delights in each other very intense.

Communion with the Father in love, with the Son in grace, and with the Holy Ghost in consolation is the high and unspeakable privilege of all the saints.[266] The Father communes with us through the Son; the Son from the Father; the Holy Ghost from both. The Father opens all the treasures of his love to us in Christ. 'Tis from off the mercy-seat he communes with us.[267] The Son opens his heart according to the pattern-love of the Father, having loved us as the Father hath loved him.[268] And the Holy Ghost opens his grace as proceeding from both, and co-equal with both as these three are one.[269] One in essence and so one in love. The love of God our Father in election, of Christ our husband in redemption, and of the Holy Ghost our Comforter in special vocation as co-equal wonders of grace are gloriously opened to the saints in their walk with God.

He, saith our Lord, that loveth me and keepeth my commandments (believing in my person as his only way to walk with God and in me walking in all the paths of obedience) shall be loved of my Father, and

---

[261] Proverbs 13:20.
[262] James 2:23; John 15:14.
[263] 2 Corinthians 6:18.
[264] Isaiah 62:5.
[265] John 14:16; Acts 9:31.
[266] 2 Corinthians 13–14.
[267] Romans 8:39; Exodus 25:22.
[268] John 15:9.
[269] 1 John 5:7.

Part I: Walking with God

I will love him, and we will come and make our abode with him.[270] And all this love-communion is carried on by the Holy Spirit, who, as our Comforter, abides with us forever and takes of the things of Christ and of the Father and shows them unto us.[271] 'Tis he directs our hearts into the love of God.[272] And O the glories of divine love, which are opened to the saints in their walking with God in Christ! …

Lord, says the soul, what manner of love is thine! Is it me thou call it a dear son! And a pleasant child whom thou wilt surely have mercy upon, who am the very worst of all thy children, and no more worthy to be called thy son.[273] Aye, says the Lord, thou art my dear child, notwithstanding all thy unkindness. And my grace is sufficient for thee,[274] sufficient to pardon, pity, strengthen, and at last completely to deliver thee. And then what admirings of grace doth the soul break forth into! "Grace, grace" is its cry![275] How unspeakably doth it rejoice in hope of the glory of God![276] In believing views of that state into which nothing that defileth can enter[277] when mortality shall be swallowed up of life.[278]

Lord, says the soul, then I shall love thee and serve thee as I would.[279] Then I'll bless thy name forever, for all thy loving-kindness, when my heart is wound up to the highest pitch of holiness.[280] Meanwhile, pardon my shortness, pity my weakness, and help my infirmities, though I think myself the most ungrateful of all thy children, thy kindness and my unkindness being set together. Yet, Lord, since thy grace is sufficient for me, even for me, I'll go on rejoicing and glorying in it as distinguishing, free, full, eternal, even while I loath myself in my own sight for all my abominations.[281]

---

[270] John 14:15, 22, 23; 15:7, 14.
[271] John 16:14–15.
[272] 2 Thessalonians 3:5.
[273] Luke 15:19.
[274] 2 Corinthians 12:9.
[275] Zechariah 4:7.
[276] Romans 5:2.
[277] Revelation 21:27.
[278] 2 Corinthians 5:4.
[279] Revelation 22:33:.
[280] Psalm 145:1.
[281] Ezekiel 20:43.

This is a little of the talk God and his people have with each other while walking together in Christ; and as they commune with each other in Christ, the great way, so in all the lesser paths comprehended in him.

In the way of faith or divine revelation, they sweetly walk and talk together as friends: I call you not servants but friends, saith our Lord, for the servant knoweth not what his Lord doeth, but all things that I have heard of my Father, I have made known unto you.[282] The gospel in all its glorious doctrines is a hidden mystery to them that are lost, notwithstanding the external revelation of it in the written Word.[283] But God herein not only walks with his own in peculiar favour, opening to them his mind by the internal revelation of his Spirit, so as that they know the truth as it is in Jesus is to be walked in by faith.

But he herein also talks with them in special grace, making particular applications of the truths known as concerning them individually, so that they not only know the truth, but the truth makes them free.[284] They know it for themselves, and their hearts burn within them while the Lord talks with them about it, opening to them the Scriptures.[285] The saints' knowledge of gospel-mysteries is fellowship-knowledge.[286]

A sameness of intention, design, or end

In the fifth and last place, a sameness of intention, design, or end. Persons here among men walking together have often the same end in view.[287] But God and his people always have.

God's end in walking with his people in Christ and in all the ways of divine appointment is ultimately his own glory and subordinately their good and salvation. And this also is his people's end in walking with him. ...

And that God's glory and our salvation should be his end in walking with us is amazing grace! What an astonishing wonder is it that he that

---

[282] John 15:15.
[283] 2 Corinthians 4:3.
[284] John 8:32.
[285] Luke 24:32.
[286] Ephesians 3:9.
[287] Proverbs 1:14.

is the God of glory,[288] so far above all praise[289] that no creature can add anything to the essential glory of his perfect, self-sufficient, and immense being,[290] should nevertheless cast the rays of his glory upon the works of his hands and admit creatures to see and admire it! He might always have hid his glory in his own invisible being and never have shined into our hearts to give us the light of the knowledge thereof in the face of Jesus Christ![291]

And further, what a wonder is it that this great God—who might have glorified his wisdom, holiness, justice, power, and truth in our everlasting destruction as sinners—should nevertheless glorify his mercy and grace and all the perfections of his being in our eternal salvation! That God should walk with us, rejoicing to do us good now and to save us at the last of free sovereign favour is very amazing! And so much the more in that it is distinguishing! And when the exceeding riches of it are opened in all his kindness to us through Christ Jesus, it must needs be in the ages to come, even to an endless eternity to the praise of the glory of his grace![292] And as God's end in walking with his people in Christ and in all the ways of divine appointment is ultimately his own glory and subordinately their good and salvation, so also this is their end in walking with him.

The saints walk with God by faith in Christ, not only for their own safety but also for his glory. When they bow the knee at the name of Jesus and confess that Christ is Lord, it's to the glory of God the Father.[293] The new nature in their souls is of the same mind with Christ who did not seek his own glory but his Father's that sent him.[294] And those saints that walk the closest with God do most regard his glory as their end. If they are filled with the fruits of righteousness, which are by Christ Jesus (whether as to faith or holiness), 'tis to the glory and praise

---

[288] Acts 7:2.
[289] Nehemiah 9:5.
[290] Job 35:7; Hebrews 11:6.
[291] Colossians 1:15; 2 Corinthians 4:6.
[292] Ephesians 2:7; 1:6.
[293] Philippians 2:10–11.
[294] John 8:50; 7:18.

of God.[295] Christ proposes this as the highest end of his people's obedience. "Herein," says he, "is my Father glorified, that ye bring forth much fruit."[296] And being married unto Christ, their risen, ever living husband, they bring forth fruit unto God. …[297]

And as the glory of God is the saints' highest end in walking with him, so if he'll please to glorify himself in them and by them, they have the highest joy. Yea, this alone, sometimes, holds the hearts of God's people to walk with him in ordinances and duties when they find no sensible benefit thereby to themselves. Thus, oft-times the soul reasons, God has made it my duty to walk with him here for his glory, and if he may be glorified, though I am not comforted, I'll go on to walk with him still.

Again, as God's glory is the ultimate end, the saints have in their eye in walking with him, so also their own good as a subordinate end is regarded by them. God not only gives us leave but has made it our duty to walk in all his ways and keep his commandments for our good.[298] "Praise ye the Lord," says the Psalmist, for it is good, yea, pleasant,[299] to walk with God all manner of ways; [it] is natively sweet to the new creature. To be spiritually minded is the saint's life.[300] They draw near to God because it's good for them.[301] And when they are near him, they say with Peter, "It's good to be here."[302] And as in their whole walk, whatever they do, they do all to the glory of God[303] that God in all things may be glorified.[304] And likewise for their own present good, so also with regard to their eternal salvation.

The salvation of their souls is the end of their faith,[305] not only eventually, but designedly. And as God and his people have a sameness of

---

[295] Philippians 1:11.
[296] John 15:8.
[297] Romans 7:4.
[298] Deuteronomy 10:12–13.
[299] Psalm 147:1.
[300] Romans 8:6.
[301] Psalm 73:28.
[302] Matthew 17:4.
[303] 1 Corinthians 10:31.
[304] 1 Peter 4:11.
[305] 1 Peter 1:9.

end in these respects in their walking with each other, so they assuredly do and shall attain it. ...

Conclusion

And that God and a creature, God and a sinner, should walk together in agreement, familiarly as friends; that Christ should be their way in his person, office, and work; that herein they should go on continually with each other, maintaining free communion and mutual fellowship, and in all, regard the same end, is such a mystery of godliness that without controversy is very great![306] The Lord's doing and marvellous in our eyes![307] And this honour have all the saints. Praise ye the Lord.[308]

---

[306] 1 Timothy 3:16.
[307] Psalm 118:23.
[308] Psalm 149:9.

PART II
Letters on Spiritual Subjects and Diverse Occasions; Sent to Relations and Friends

*"I have no doubt, my dear child,
[that] you have already come unto Christ for life.
But I want you to come repeatedly, and to come with freedom."*
– Letter XXI

Provenance

Anne Dutton's cherished ministry was to write letters to specific believers and offer them encouragement and biblical counsel, especially those recently converted, struggling with their faith, or facing trial in their Christian journey. Evident in her letters was her compassion for disheartened Christians. She was regarded as a trusted guide, godly and wise, her letter-writing solicited by individuals and supported by leaders like George Whitefield.

An impressive collection of these spiritual letters is available to readers today owing to Dutton herself who tirelessly copied the private letters so that other Christians could benefit from them and publishers who sought to have them printed. The publications of her *Letters on Spiritual Subjects* (her "Letter-Books") first appeared in 1740 at the time of the Evangelical Revival. There are about 22 volumes of these Letter-Books,[1] comprising letters written to family, friends, ministers or lay people in the church, and church communities.

The following letter excerpts are from Dutton's 1747 publication *Letters on Spiritual Subjects and Diverse Occasions; Sent to Relations and Friends*, her fifth Letter-Book.[2] In a journal entry dated June 21, 1747, Dutton writes, "I sent my fifth volume of letters to the press. When I was about to send it, I thought it my duty to seek the Lord for his blessing."[3] Perceiving her own sinfulness upon sending it out, Dutton recalls Isaiah 6:7–8: "I was encouraged by this, *Whom shall I send, and who will go for us?* to hope that the Lord had some service to be done for his dear children by my poor little book and humbly entreated

---

[1] Sciretti, "Anne Dutton as a Spiritual Director," 31. See also Sciretti, "Feed My Lambs," 347.
[2] See Sciretti, "Feed My Lambs," 350.
[3] Watson, *Autobiography*, 224.

him to send me thereby to do it, that his blessing might attend this my feeble attempt for his glory and the good of his people."[4] Dutton desired, above all, to glorify God through her epistolary ministry and humbly relied on his sovereignty for its outcome.

Characteristic of many of the covers of her publications, the author is first identified by the inscription, "By One who has tasted that the Lord is Gracious," and then, "By Mrs Dutton of Great Gransden, Huntingdonshire."[5] The scripture that follows reflects Dutton's mission in her letters to correspondents: "Wherefore comfort yourselves together, and edify one another, even as also ye do, 1 Thess. v. 11." Since spiritual edification was Dutton's primary purpose for copying her letters, dates are not indicated in the printed publications nor the names of recipients (other than their initials).[6] Historical context, therefore, cannot be definitively established since the letters could have been written years before publication; and while some names can be uncovered, most remain unidentifiable.

This fifth Letter-Book contains 44 letters, 20 addressed to males and 20 to females (including her parents and brother); one to a couple (Rev. Jonathan Barber and his wife from Bethesda[7]); and three to Methodist communities which include Bethesda, Northampton, and Olney. The letters show that individuals wrote to Dutton on a variety of topics, and to each of these letters she replies with the utmost candour, care, and Christ-centered counsel.

The inclusion of the subsequent selection of letters (some of which are presented in their entirety and some in excerpts) aims to provide the reader with a sense of Dutton's letter ministry in terms of its breadth and depth and, of course, an occasion to receive gospel-saturated counsel on matters that continue to concern Christians today.

---

[4] Watson, *Anne Dutton Autobiography*, 224.
[5] Dutton copying her letters and publishing them during her lifetime was a rare practice, and she faced criticism for it, even more for doing so being a woman. Many of her publications have only her initials. See Sciretti, "Feed My Lambs," 345.
[6] Sciretti, "Feed My Lambs," 347–49.
[7] Sciretti, "Feed My Lambs," 374.

2
Death and the Joys of Heaven

LETTER II. To Mr. W--------s.[1]

Ever dear and honoured Father,

Yours I received with much concern to hear that my dear mother was so weak. I sympathize with you, my dear father, in your present affliction.

May the Lord sanctify it for your soul's advantage! We live in a world where sin, sorrow, and death abide. All our pleasures here are short-lived and are sometimes dashed with unpleasing mixtures. In the world we go to, holiness, joy, and life—perfect and eternal—reign. Pleasures immixed in new and ever-living joys, proceeding from the throne of God and of the Lamb, incessantly and ineffably delight the inhabitants of the upper world.

Let us not mourn for our dearest relatives when God calls them home to himself as if their joy was not full that are gone before us, nor as if our sorrow was perpetual that are left behind them. Let the joy of their gain who are called to be with Christ alleviate the grief for our loss which is apt to attend us when the desire of our eyes is taken away with a stroke. And for ourselves, since the time is short, let us mourn as if we mourned not.

As strangers and pilgrims on earth, let our thoughts and joys be in heaven. And as got far on our way through the wilderness towards Canaan's land, let our hasty feet, the affections of our souls, move the faster when we see any of our dear companions passing over Jordan before us. Yet a little while and we also shall be loved home to be forever

---

[1] Williams is Dutton's maiden name. Dutton writes this letter to her father Mr. Williams.

with the Lord—to see him as he is, to love and serve him in perfection and without interruption to a blessed eternity.

Then we shall bid adieu to a wicked heart, a tempting devil, and an ensnaring world. And no more shall a weak or a diseased body trouble us. No hindrance then as to our enjoyment of God or employment for him, [for²] these things shall any more attend us. The inhabitant of that city, which our God hath prepared for us, shall say, "No more I am sick," either as to soul or body. Mortality respecting our souls shall be swallowed up of life immediately upon the dissolution of our earthly tabernacles and respecting our bodies at the resurrection of the just.

In patience then let us possess our souls while we live and in well-doing commit the keeping of them to God as unto a faithful Creator who will perfect that which concerneth us. And when we die, in our last acts of faith, let us say with Stephen, "Lord Jesus, receive my spirit,"³ and cheerfully commit our bodies to his care to sleep a while in their duty beds perfumed for them by our Lord's lying in the grave until he shall say at the resurrection-morn, "Awake and sing, ye that dwell in dust,"⁴ and thereby raise us up into eternal glory with him.

Wishing the consolations of God may abound towards you and requesting your prayers, I subscribe, my honoured father,

Your most obedient child,

---

² Corrected from *from*
³ Acts 7:59.
⁴ Isaiah 26:19.

3
Discouragement in Pastoral Ministry

LETTER VII. To Mr. B-------r.[1]

Honoured and very dear brother in Christ, your Lord and mine, in him I greet you, wishing grace and peace. Amen.

... As to your inward trials, my dear brother, I feel an inward sympathy with you; I bring you and your case before the God of compassions and pray him to succour[2] and relieve you. Oh, my dear brother, "Be strong, yea, be strong."[3] Jesus is with you in your work; his grace is sufficient for you, and his power shall rest upon you. Oh, cast the burden of all your labour upon the Lord, and he will sustain you. Christ hath a mighty shoulder, though your arm is weak. Continue, my dear brother, to feed your Lord's sheep and lambs at Bethesda[4] while he fixeth your abode amongst them and to take the oversight of them as you have hitherto done, not by constraint but of a ready mind. "And when the chief shepherd shall appear, you shall receive a crown of glory which fadeth not away."[5]

What are your momentary troubles to your eternal crown! What is that weight of present care that is on you with respect to their souls if compared with that far more exceeding and eternal weight of glory

---

[1] This is Jonathan Barber, the spiritual director of Bethesda, George Whitefield's orphan house in Georgia. Sciretti, "Feed My Lambs," 251.

[2] Meaning, "To help; to assist in difficulty or distress; to relieve." Johnson, Samuel. "succour." *A Dictionary of the English Language*, https://johnsonsdictionaryonline.com/1755/succour_va. Accessed June 18, 2023.

[3] Daniel 10:19.

[4] Whitefield encouraged and entreated Dutton to use her gifts of writing to minister to the Bethesda community. In one letter, Whitefield had informed Dutton that her *Walking with God* had been a blessing to his friends and others in the American colonies. Dutton would devote herself faithfully to this overseas correspondence. See Sciretti, "Feed My Lambs," 246–252.

[5] 1 Peter 5:4.

which is reserved for you as a labourer for their good in the gospel of Christ! Is not the one light, very light, if compared with the other?

Come, my brother: it is for Christ you labour and bear the heat and burden of the day. It is for him that loved you and washed you from your sins in his own blood. It is for him, who, though the Lord of glory, humbled himself and became a servant for you. That obeyed and suffered, that laboured and cared, that was mocked and scourged, that sweat and bled, that died and rose, that lives and reigns for you! Oh, consider what vast obligations the love of Christ lays you under, and I am sure you will think you can never do enough in duty and gratitude for him.

Again, consider it is your Lord's sheep and lambs for which you labour. And what you do for them, he will take it as done to himself. And while the voice of Christ to you is,

Lovest thou me?
Feed my lambs.
Lovest thou me?
Feed my sheep.

Oh, what an endearment doth it bring with it to the lambs and sheep of Jesus, the good, the great, the glorious shepherd! I am sure, my dear brother, when Jesus speaks to your heart, and, putting it upon your love to him, bids you feed his lambs, he puts them into your heart thereby and draws out your bowels toward them in such sort that you would gladly spend your whole life to serve them.

"Aye," perhaps you'll say, "so I would. I would gladly spend and be spent for their good and salvation. But I am so poor a servant, can do so little for them, and am of so little use to them that this is a greater burden to me than all my work."

Oh, my brother, let the burden of your own weakness and insufficiency rest on your Lord's strength and all-sufficiency. The fullness of Christ is yours to supply your every want in your every time of need.

Part II: Letters on Spiritual Subjects and Diverse Occasions

Let not a sense of want distress you but only excite you to be the more intimately free with the fullness of Christ who filleth all in all.

Go tell the Lord Jesus your whole heart as soon as ever any distress breaks in upon your spirit. Hide not yourself from your best friend, from your brother Jesus, who was born for your adversity, on purpose, that he might sympathize with you in it, succour and relieve you under it, and deliver you from it; who loves you as himself, as his own flesh; who hath all power to help you and all grace and faithfulness to do it.

Oh, lay your weary head in Christ's bosom. There is room for you. You shall be welcome; yea, a joy will it be to your Lord to see you thus free with him. He died that he might bring you near. Oh, stand not at a distance but lean upon Jesus's breast. And there take a holy ease from all anxious care and perplexing thought until, refreshed with his bosom love, he says unto you with a life-giving, a strength-creating voice, "Go, my dear servant. Go do this and that work for me. 'Fear not, thou worm Jacob, for I am with thee. Be not dismayed, for I am thy God. I will strengthen thee; yea, I will help thee; yea, I will uphold thee with the right hand of my righteousness.'"[6]

I mean not by this, my dear brother, to deter you from any duty till you feel strength for it, but to excite you to rest by faith in Christ's bosom in the way of your duty until by his all-efficacious voice he enables you cheerfully to perform it. For most assuredly will he comfort your disconsolate soul and strengthen you when you have no might so that you shall "mount up with wings as eagles, you shall run and not be weary and shall walk and not faint."[7] Thus, cast the burden of your weakness upon the Lord until he strengthens you for your work.

And if this discouragement should press in upon your spirit to burden your mind, "That you are but of little use in the performance thereof," cast that also upon the Lord. Your work is with the Lord, and your reward is with your God. Your labour is with the Lord. He strictly regards and will richly reward all the work you do for him according to

---

[6] Isaiah 41:14, 10.
[7] Isaiah 40:31.

the labour you take in his service, singly and alone considered as well as according to the fruit of your doings.

And your labour in Christ's gospel may be attended with more abundant fruit than you at present know of. You do not, will not, know all the fruits of your present labours until that day when the secrets of all hearts shall be opened, and the Lord, your royal master of the freest grace, shall bring forth all that has been done for him by you, known and unknown to you, unto praise and honour and glory. While with a "Well done, good and faithful servant," he bids you "enter into the joy of your Lord."[8]

And let me say, not only is all your labour and the fruit of it strictly regarded and will be richly rewarded, but also that which you would have done for Christ therein. Your willing mind, the desires of your soul to serve the Lord Jesus in all those extensive degrees which your heart has ever breathed after is accepted, accounted as your kindness, as your being holiness to the Lord in his service and shall accordingly be rewarded by him.

Add to these considerations the glory of your present work, which of grace unknown is given you and the greatness of your future reward. And what room is there for you, as a servant of Christ, to be in heaviness? Or rather, what cause have you not as such, of all joy and triumph in your glorious master and his blessed work! "Be strong," therefore, my dear brother, "and of a good courage, for the Lord your God will not fail you nor forsake you."[9]

And though now and then for a season you should be suffered to be in heaviness, yet even *this* shall be overruled by your master's power and grace to fit you more for some parts of your work: as sympathy with others in like distress; fitness to speak a word in season to weary, tempted souls and to comfort them that are in any trouble with the same comforts wherewith you yourself are comforted of God in all your tribulations. And thus, you shall be the more prepared for your crown.

---

[8] Matthew 25:23.
[9] Deuteronomy 31:6.

Part II: Letters on Spiritual Subjects and Diverse Occasions

Yea, the more temptations you endure while you abide with Christ in his service, the greater will be the glory of your reward. You shall be crowned as an overcomer and shortly will your Lord grant unto you to sit with him in his throne, even as he also overcame and is set down with his Father in his throne. Endure hardness then, my beloved brother, as a good soldier of Jesus Christ. Unto his grace, I commit you.

… Oh, my dear brother, our Lord's mighty shoulder bears us and all our load, or soon we should sink into nothing, or, as you say, into "inconceivable misery."

And it is brave bearing of burdens with the Rock of Ages beneath us while we and our loads are both borne by omnipotence. And the weights we feel that would crush us into death serve as an opportunity for the Lord our life to refresh our souls with the sweet breezes of his infinite favour by the Holy Ghost, the Comforter, which fill us with joy unspeakable here and prepare us for glory eternal hereafter.

I remember you before the Lord. Pray and give thanks for, dear Sir,
Yours most affectionately in Jesus,

4
Walking by Faith Amidst Trial

LETTER IX. To the dear family at Bethesda.[1]

Honoured and very dear brethren,

I rejoiced for your joy in that bright shine of the sun of righteousness which was cast on your dear souls in the beginning of March 1743–4 as soon as we received the good news of those salvation-wonders which the Lord wrought amongst you. Oh, what a joyful spring, my dear brethren and sisters, was it with you then! The time of singing of birds unto you was come. And it came as an earnest of that everlasting spring, that eternal summer which awaits you, and of those everlasting songs of praise unto God and to the Lamb, which you shall incessantly sing when, as the ransomed of the Lord, you shall be brought unto Zion above, with everlasting joy upon your heads, and sorrow and sighing shall flee away.

And though since then, the light of God's countenance hath been in some measure withdrawn, and an autumn has succeeded your pleasant spring, yet let none of you doubt the Lord's work for and upon you when you enjoyed his sweet presence and was filled with all joy and peace in believing. Nor yet be you afraid that the Lord will return no more to your dear souls.

Oh, you dear lambs of Christ, the Lord your Shepherd is Jesus Christ, the same yesterday, and today, and forever. The very same that he said unto you at the beginning. If the love of his heart towards you

---

[1] Whitefield's orphan house in Savannah, Georgia. Dutton was esteemed as a spiritual advisor there. Writing in the fall of 1744, Dutton reassures the Bethesda community during a time when they are feeling low in spirits, not witnessing the salvation fruits they experienced earlier. See Sciretti, "Feed My Lambs," 252, 381.

had not been infinitely great and immensely free, if it had not been a sin-pardoning, a grace-giving, and a glory-bestowing love that was well able to save you to the uttermost, he would not have told you of his loving-kindness when you lay distressed under a sense of your own sins and vileness. The Lord's showing you your misery by sin and enabling you to hope in his mercy was his manifesting himself unto you as he doth not unto the world.

You were Christ's own and loved by him with an everlasting love, or you had not been drawn with loving-kindness in that day of his power upon your hearts when you was first made willing to receive Christ as your Saviour, as your Lord, your love, your life, your all, and to give up yourselves to him to be saved by him from all sin and misery unto all grace and glory. And, having loved you as his own, he will love you to the end forever, freely, unchangeably, and eternally. Your beloved is not gone. He only standeth as it were behind your wall to hear with pleasure how you will cry after him while his own hand draws out your hearts to seek him.

And don't he now and then look forth upon you through the windows of the promises and show himself unto you through the lattice[2] of his ordinances? Oh, wait a while, a little while longer, and you shall see your Lord again, and your hearts shall rejoice, and your joy shall no man take from you. You shall have spring after spring. The bright sun of eternal love shall break out upon you with renewed shines after intervening clouds. Until that day comes, when clouds and darkness shall be no more but in an everlasting shine of infinite favour, the Lord shall be your everlasting light and your God, your glory.

And you, the dear sheep of Jesus, who have had long experience of your Shepherd's care and kindness, oh, don't you doubt his love or say you know him not, lest you be liars like unto Satan who suggests the same to you. But led by Jesus, follow him in all the paths of duty until you are brought to glory. Walk by faith now; you shall shortly live by sight. You have but a little time left to glorify God in by believing in the

---

[2] Corrected from *lattess*.

dark. See that you improve it, for blessed eternity comes on when faith shall be turned into vision. And when you're in the light of glory, you will be glad of every act of faith that ever you put forth upon God and Christ while you walked in the darkness which attends this vale of misery. Inasmuch as thereby you glorified God upon the earth, covet therefore now, you dearly beloved, of the Lord to give him such a glory by believing through a thousand difficulties as you cannot give him when trials shall forever cease when all sorrow and death shall be swallowed up of joy and life eternal.

    I cease not to pray for you.

    Wishing all prosperity, I leave you in the arms of Jesus.

    Pray for, my dear brethren,

    Your most affectionate friend and servant,

    In our glorious Lord,

5
God's Providence in Prosperity and Adversity

LETTER XII. To Mr. and Mrs. W-------s[1]

Dear and honoured parents,

Oh, how good is our God! How good is he and will he be to us, the objects of his special love? Verily it shall be as he hath said, "My people shall be satisfied with my goodness."[2] Oh, how hath goodness and mercy followed us all along hitherto! And all the days of our present life will they still follow us until, by goodness and mercy in the stream, we are wafted into the ocean, into the full enjoyment of God in life eternal.

How kind are all the Lord's dealings with us? All are towards us, goodness; towards us, mercy. When he hides and chides, he loves as well as when he smiles and embraceth us. It is the same infinite love of our unchanging God that flows in every channel, whether in the pure and native displays of loving kindness or clothed with the veil of his fatherly rebukes. Whatever our God is doing with us, he is always loving and saving us—when he crosseth our desires as well as when he grants them. It is but if need be that we are in heaviness through manifold temptations. The gracious design of our heavenly Father, in all his chastisements, is to make us partakers of his holiness.

Nor shall our trials always abide. No, God's fatherly anger in providential frowns is for a moment, but in his favour is life. Weeping may endure for a night, but joy cometh in the morning. And, the day is his;

---

[1] Mr. and Mrs. Williams, Dutton's parents.
[2] Jeremiah 31:14.

the night also is his. The day of our prosperity is the Lord's, of his appointing, for his glory and our good; and the night of our adversity is likewise his. And the measure of light in the one and of darkness in the other, with the length of both, are also of his appointing for holy, wise, and gracious ends. And in and for both is his holy name to be praised while day and night in providential frowns and smiles alternately succeed each other until night and darkness are swallowed up in eternal day. For all things work together for our good, according to the power and grace of our all-wise God.

How cheerfully then in faith should we receive all things from the hand of the Lord? And how humbly and obedientially in love should we walk before him who are so greatly beloved of him? The good will of him that dwelt in the bush be with you.[3] Pray, my honoured parents, for

Yours most obediently,

---

[3] Deuteronomy 33:16.

6
Fearing that One's Spiritual State Is the Result of a Pious Education and Therefore Not Saving

LETTER XIII. To Mr. A-------n.

My dear brother in the Lord,

Yours I received and give you thanks for it. The account you gave me of the Lord's work upon your soul refresheth my spirit, and that he was pleased to make my printed account of his gracious dealings with me a comfort unto you as you found so great a part of it to answer to your own experience, for which I rejoice and bless the Lord.[1]…

I would next attempt a short answer to those objections which arise in your mind and make you fear that the Lord's work on your soul is not saving, or whether it be any more than the fruit of a pious education.

But before I consider your objections in particular, let me say, a pious education is a great privilege, a means to restrain from vice and immorality and to train up youth in a doctrinal knowledge of the truths of the gospel and is often blessed for conviction and may be for conversion.

But the most pious education that ever any person was favoured with, as in and of itself, never did nor can give such a spiritual conviction of sin, of heart-sin, as to make the soul cry out in the views of the uncleanness of its nature in the light of the law's spirituality and of its

---

[1] Dutton proceeds to answer this man's first inquiry regarding whether or not the work of God upon his soul is truly a work of grace by giving him six theological considerations. Her counsel is echoed in her 1761 London publication, *The Marks of a Child of God*.

own inability to help or save itself. Woe is me, for I am undone! Nor yet did the most pious education, as in and of itself, ever make Christ precious as the only and all-sufficient Saviour unto any one soul.

No, these are, as I may say, the two main hinges upon which the soul turns from a state of nature to a state of grace. They are the two great characters whereby a new creature, a man that is in Christ, may be known and the undeniable evidences of a real, spiritual, gracious change upon the heart or of the soul's being brought out of nature's darkness into God's marvelous light.

Such a man is new-made, hath true, precious faith, the faith of God's elect, wrought in his heart unto which the everlasting salvation of the soul is annexed. And the power that produced it was not the natural force of a pious education but the supernatural power and almighty energy of the Holy Ghost in regeneration. The most pious education is a tree of too low a nature to bear such high and precious fruits. …

But I must come to your objections. And you fear the work of God upon your soul is not saving and say,

Objection I:[2]   Because I have not felt those terrors of conscience for sin that others have.

Answer: The same degree of terror is not necessary to be felt by every soul that is truly convinced of sin, nor is it usual for those who have had a pious education and been restrained from outward immoralities to feel the same degree of terror as those who have run great lengths in wicked courses. If a moralized person that has been religiously educated hath had so much terror for sin for his heart and life-sin that he dares not trust in himself or in his own doings for life, but, being warned of God

---

[2] Not included in this letter: "Objection II. Because I have not experienced those overflowing joys in believing, which other saints have"; "Objection III. Because I have not those inward troubles and temptations from Satan, which other Christians have"; and "Objection IV. Because the work of God has been so gradual upon my soul."

by his holy law of the wrath which is to come and by his gospel of fleeing unto Christ as the only hiding place from it and being moved with fear (of being found out of Christ), runs into him for safety—it is sufficient to prove a saving conviction of sin.

And as great a display of the power of the Holy Ghost in his work of convincing of sin is this where the soul hath less terror as where the same work in other souls that have been openly immoral is attended with greater terrors. I humbly think that the display of power in the former is the greatest.

But, however, the glories of omnipotence, in various rays, shine in both. The soul that hath passed under the greatest terrors, which have been overruled to bring him to Christ hath cause to bless God forever, for his kind dealings with him in that though he led him by a rough way, he brought him to such a glorious place of rest and safety.

And the soul that hath had less terror, that is not left to rest short of Christ, is equally safe with the other and hath reason in a particular manner to bless God that he gave him such an easy passage from his soul-pursuers into Christ, the city of refuge, and brought him through the straits of the new-birth without those pangs and throws which some souls feel.

Which way soever the Lord deals with us in conviction of sin, he leads us by a right way that is and shall be most for his glory and our joy if we are brought thereby unto Christ, that city of habitation....

As to these objections, my brother, which arise in your mind, and many more of a like nature, which at times perplex the hearts of God's people—there is no just ground for them. Inasmuch as the things objected, as wanting in some particular souls which are to be found in others truly gracious, belong not to the essentials of a state of grace but to the circumstantials which, with much difference in different persons, attend gracious souls. If we would judge of our state of grace by comparing our experience with that of others whom we look upon to be truly gracious, let us do it in those generals wherein all agree, and not in particulars, in which there is so much difference. …

It appears to me, my brother, that you [were] a regenerate soul when what the world calls innocent diversion became so disagreeable to you that what was your former chief delight became your greatest burden. The cause, as I conceive, was this: the new-nature was wrought in your soul, a holy, spiritual appetite that could find no delight in natural, sinful pleasures but still fought pleasures of a higher kind, of a heavenly extraction, agreeable to itself, and its heavenly descent and taste, with which alone it could be satisfied.

This is evidenced to me by that pleasure which you then found in heart-mourning for sin; by that fear which you then had, lest convictions should wear off without any saving effect; by your desire after deeper convictions of sin; and by your earnest prayer for grace to live a holy life here if you never might enjoy happiness hereafter. These things, together with what you have experienced since, make the work of God upon your soul appear to me very clear and full, that it is indeed a real, supernatural work of divine grace which is wrought in none but those who are prepared for glory, or made meet to be partakers of the inheritance of the saints in light. …

Grace be with you! In the arms of Christ I leave you, and am, dear Sir,

> Most affectionately yours in him,

7

Doubting One's Own Interest in Christ When Considering One's Restraint in Proclaiming Christ

LETTER XVIII. To Mr. W-------t.

My dear brother in Christ,

I am glad you have blessed experience of the things you tell me of. And I am well persuaded that the work of God upon your soul is a saving work of the Holy Spirit.

As to the things you mention which make you fear that the work of God on your heart is not saving, I would just give a hint or two.

And first. As to "Your not speaking of the loveliness of Christ to others as some Christians do" while you abide under fear about your own interest in him that restrains your spirit.

But remember that of those that fear the Lord, that have faith in him and love to him or the true reverence of him in their hearts, there are two sorts:

As 1. Those that speak often one to another.

And 2. Those that think upon his name.

That [have not] that freedom of speech which others have but are on several accounts restrained from speaking for the Lord and have only liberty to think upon his name.[1] And to this latter sort, the Saviour's bowels yearn, even to those who can only think upon his name, that inwardly say of Christ, "He is precious," that love and cleave to him in his person, in his relations, in his offices, in his people, in his Word

---

[1] Malachi 3:16.

and ordinances. And for these, a book of remembrance is written before him. The Lord hearkens and hears with infinite pleasure and records in infinite grace what is the language of their hearts concerning him as well as what is the voice of others' lips. The thoughts of the one and the words of the other, even all that both ways is said of him by those that fear him is written down before him. "And they shall be mine," saith the Lord of hosts, "in that day when I make up my jewels."[2]

Now then, my dear brother, if you are at present one of this latter sort that can only think of Christ and can't yet speak boldly for him as others do, don't yield to fear that you are not the Lord's on this account. Since he himself says concerning you that you are one of his jewels and that you shall be his in that day when he makes them up. That is, you shall then openly appear to be the Lord's, to be one of the jewels on which his heart is fixed by that visible glory, that amazing luster, which he'll then put upon you according to that secret relation which you now bear to him and that gracious estimation which he now hath of you.

This I say to encourage your hope in Christ as to your relation to him though but a thinker of him, but not to hinder your speaking for him. No, speak as you can; tell others what you think of Christ.

Set forth the beauties you have seen in him; lisp them out if it be but with a stammering tongue, and although attended with a thousand fears as to your own interest in this glorious object, yet commend him to others to draw other souls to fall in love with the altogether lovely Jesus. For hereby your Lord will be glorified, his people edified, and your own soul enlarged. ...

Yet my dear brother, by your keeping silence, you come short of that glory of God which you ought to give him in your life. The Lord says of his people, "Ye are my witnesses." This he esteems his glory, and truly it is theirs to bear a becoming testimony for God and his truths before all. It is most surely our duty as opportunity offers in meekness of wisdom to speak of the greatness and goodness of God and of the evil and danger of sin; of the greatness of his grace toward repenting sinners;

---

[2] Malachi 3:17.

and of the greatness of his wrath that shall be made known on the impenitent.

And this we ought to do, both in love to God and man. In love to God, we should do what in us lies to stem that tide of ungodliness which runs down our streets like a mighty torrent. And in love to man ought we to warn him of that pit of misery which he is sliding into by every sin. And especially ought we to do this since it is God's express command: "Thou shalt not hate thy brother in thine heart; thou shalt in any wise rebuke thy neighbour, and not suffer sin upon him."[3] Nor can we omit this duty without making ourselves guilty and in some sort partakers of other men's sins.

But, my brother, though we sin daily, both by omission and commission, yet our heavenly Father forgives us and will still call us his dear children, although in many things we behave very unlike them, which should be the matter of our constant humiliation before him, but not of an unbelieving departure from him. We should not doubt our sonship because we fail in our duty; but believing our relation, we should humble ourselves for our transgression, confess our sins over the head of the great sacrifice, and seek to our Father for more grace to enable us to live more to his glory, to cleanse ourselves from all filthiness, both of flesh and spirit, and to perfect holiness in his fear.

In a word, my brother, whatever part of obedience to Christ you see lovely in other believers, which you mourn the want of in yourself, instead of doubting the truth of your own faith thereby, instantly follow theirs. Follow them as they follow Christ. And be sure to leave no duty undone, at least unattempted by the neglect of which you are put to doubt whether you are a child of God or not. Walk by faith in Christ and in all the paths of obedience by love, so shall your joy be full here and your glory great hereafter.

My dear brother, unto what I have said in answer to your letter, allow me to add that the best way to get satisfaction of your interest in Christ and of the truth of a work of special grace on your heart is to

---

[3] Leviticus 19:17.

venture on the Saviour daily as a poor perishing sinner in yourself and instantly to take him at his Word, that so believing on him, coming, looking to him, you shall be saved by him—even before you see the fruits of this your faith in the increase of love and every other grace. Nothing glorifies God like a life of faith on Christ continually. And nothing like this brings increase of grace and holiness, of joy and glory to the soul.

Every fresh act of faith on Christ strengthens the habit, the principle of faith in the soul. And as your faith hereby will increase, so your love and every grace will accordingly abound in your heart and life. Let your faith on Christ be as God hath appointed it, the prime evidence of your interest in him, and your obedience of love to him a subordinate evidence. Then will the motions of your soul to Christ and for him be regular, and your joy in him and his salvation full and perpetual.

To the tender compassions of our great high priest, I commit you; and with sympathizing love, am, dear Sir,

Yours in Christ,

8
Guilt over One's Sins and Coming unto Christ with Freedom

LETTER XXI. To Mrs. R--------ll.

My dear sister in our precious Jesus,

... But come, my sister, come and see Jesus! Look upon the Christ of God, anointed to save sinners. He can save you to the uttermost. Come, try him, trust him, cast your soul into his arms. They are wide open to receive you. Come without fear; come and welcome to your own Lord Jesus.

What, afraid to come to him because of your guilt? He hath buried it in his own blood. Grieve your Lord no longer by your sin of unbelief, but instantly say with Thomas, "My Lord and my God!"[1] If you doubt it, put your finger into the print of the nails and thrust your hand into his side. Those wounds were made for you, that you might have access to the heart-love of your dying Lord and through him your bleeding sacrifice, unto God, as the God of peace.

The work is done, my sister: peace for you is made by the blood of Jesus. Stand not numbering over your numberless transgressions. The Lord hath blotted them out for his own sake and will not remember your sins.[2] Know you not that it is God's covenant with us sinners, through his bleeding Son, that he will be merciful to our unrighteousness and remember our sins no more?

Do you want to know your interest in God's everlasting covenant? Lay hold on it: stretch out the hand of faith to lay hold of this grace. It

---

[1] John 20:28.
[2] Isaiah 43:25.

is holden forth to sinners, the very chief. You can but be a sinner, the chief of sinners. Muster up all the sins you can think of: the sin of your nature and practice, of your heart and ways.

And as a chief sinner, come lay hold of all the grace exhibited in the Saviour. There is an infinite all-sufficiency in it to save you, a redundancy, a more than enough. O! Cast yourself into a sea of grace, prepared for you by the Lamb's blood, and there take your fill. You have the Saviour's Word for it. That coming unto him, he will in no wise cast you out.[3] Not a soul shall die that comes. Not a soul that comes but shall be saved from all sin and misery unto all grace and glory.

The physician, Christ, can heal your deadly wounds. He is in office to save. He doth all freely. He delights to save. You cannot please him better than to come to him to be saved by him. Come show him all your griefs, your mortal wounds, your putrifying sores. His bowels will melt towards you, his compassions will flow out upon you, and from a heart inexpressibly touched with a feeling of your miseries will he stretch out his hand of mercy to save you in himself with an everlasting salvation. Yea, he will rejoice over you, thus, to do you good.

I have no doubt, my dear child, [that[4]] you have already come unto Christ for life. But I want you to come repeatedly, and to come with freedom. For this the Lord will bring you to in his own time.

The souls' coming unto Christ is to be considered in a two-fold respect.

As 1. Its coming to him by its desires, upon its discernings of his beauty, all-sufficiency, and suitableness as the only Saviour, held forth by the gospel to the chief of sinners.

And 2. Its coming by appropriation or with freedom-steps, under a delightful persuasion of interest in him.

And to both these acts of faith in the Saviour, the drawings of the Father are absolutely and previously necessary. The drawing of the

---

[3] John 6:37.
[4] Altered from *but*, meaning, "13. That...." Johnson, Samuel. "but." *A Dictionary of the English Language*, https://johnsonsdictionaryonline.com/1755/but_conj, 1755. Accessed June 18, 2023.

Part II: Letters on Spiritual Subjects and Diverse Occasions

Father in order to the souls' motion unto Christ by earnest desire consists in that inward, heart-attracting revelation which he makes of the Saviour. The drawing of the Father in order to the soul's motion unto Christ by appropriation or with freedom steps consists in that delightful persuasion which he gives the soul of its interest in the Saviour when the grace of the gospel is brought home in the sweetness of individuation ...

The first may be where the other is not. The first is *before* the other. And where the first is, the other shall be.

And upon these two distinct drawings of the Father, the soul's coming unto Christ in the two respects mentioned is founded and orderly proceeds.

Now then, my dear sister, when you feel an earnest desire after Christ, that is your soul's motion to him. And come you could not, even in this respect, unless the Father drew you by showing you the infinite excellency of that lovely, glorious object which your soul desires. And he that has begun to draw you will go on with his work of drawing until you come with freedom—to be familiar with Jesus as your beloved, as your friend, your husband, head, your life, your all.

It is this latter drawing that you want. It is this latter coming you long for and find at present an incapacity for it. But be of good cheer: by and by, the Father will draw you so strongly, with such ravishing sweetness, that you shall run with freedom under shining discoveries of your interest in Jesus to take up your rest by faith in his bosom as the sum of your delights and center of your soul. ...

Farewell in the Lord. Pray for, my dear sister,

Yours in our sweet Jesus,

9
Strengthening Against Error and Being Established in the Precious Truths of the Gospel

LETTER XXXIII.
To the remnant of the Methodist Society in N--------n,[1] who through the power of Christ resting upon them are enabled to stand in a day of shakings. Grace and peace be multiplied.

My dear and honoured brethren,

It is with great joy that I hear of your walking in the truth and with tender concern that you have had none among you lately to break the bread of life to your precious souls. I am glad that you meet twice a week. Still continue that practice to speak often one to another and unto the Lord for and with each other. For he hearkens and hears, and a book of remembrance is written before him for you who thus fear the Lord and think upon his name. And you shall be his in that day when he makes up his jewels. And mean time, the Lord will spare you as a man spareth his own Son that serveth him. Jesus will come and stand in the midst of you when you meet together and say, "Peace be unto you." He will breathe upon your souls and thereby communicate unto you the reviving, comforting influences of the Holy Ghost. Don't think, though forsaken as it were of men that used to feed you, that you are left alone. For the Lord your Saviour, whose you are and whom you serve, will never, never leave you nor forsake you. And I trust he will soon send some of his dear servants among you to feed you with the

---

[1] Northhampton society, one of the Methodist societies Dutton wrote to.

pure doctrines of his life-giving Word and to lead you to drink of the unmuddied waters of gospel-grace.

My dear brethren, you are [in] Christ's care, the sheep whom he loved and bought with his blood, the sheep whom he sought up and brought home by his power, the sheep on whom his heart-love is eternally fixed. And you shall not die for want of food so long as the Lord your Shepherd lives. No, into fat, green pastures will he lead you; beside the still, deep waters will he make you to lie down. After decays, after wanderings, he will restore your souls and lead you in the paths of righteousness for his name's sake. Yea, though you should walk through the valley of the shadow of death, you need fear no evil, for there the Lord your life is and will be with you. A table he will still prepare before you in the presence of your enemies; anoint your heads with oil and fill your cup even to running over. Most surely his goodness and mercy shall follow you, even all the days of your life. And to receive grace from him and to ascribe glory to him do you dwell in the house of the Lord forever. And say, yea, sing, my dear brethren, in faith and joy, each one for yourselves, "The Lord is my Shepherd, I shall not want feeding, healing, direction, protection, honour and joy, glory and blessing from the God of my salvation. And unto him be dominion and glory and blessing forever and ever. Amen!"

Think it not strange, my dear brethren, as if some strange thing had happened that after such a great and glorious work of God, by the gospel of truth, which hath appeared of late, in this and other nations, the Enemy, Satan, as a spirit of error, should be let loose to try the faith of many and to overthrow the faith of some. For thus it was in the Apostolic Age, even after that great and plentiful effusion of the Holy Ghost at the day of Pentecost, with which the apostles and the first Christian church for some time was so highly favoured. It is evident that the apostle John lived to see seducers in the church and wrote to confirm the saints in the true faith and to strengthen them against the errors of those who seduced them. And the apostle Jude found it necessary to write to the Christians in his day and exhort them to contend earnestly for the faith which was once delivered unto the saints, the true faith which was first taught, being opposed and reproached by men of corrupt minds. And evident it is from the writings of the other apostles that several great errors were sprung up among the saints and churches which they wrote to, which obliged them to write for the vindication and further manifestation of the truth for the discovery of error and for the confirmation of weak believers, who like little children were apt to be tossed to and fro with every wind of doctrine that were cast upon them by men of cunning craftiness. And thus it hath been from the beginning until now.

And shall we then, my dear brethren, think it strange that after such a delightful appearance of the approaching glory of Christ's kingdom in the conversion of souls by the Word of truth, which hath been seen of late, the adversary and enemy should send up such a mist of the darkness of error to obscure the brightness of the glorious gospel to stop its progress and obstruct its efficacy? No, let us mourn for the opposition made against Christ and his truth, but let us rejoice that Zion's king reigneth, that the rod, the scepter, the gospel of his strength shall yet go forth out of Zion and that his people shall yet be made his willing subjects in the day of his power. And however the Enemy with his falsehoods hath prevailed and may for a time proceed, most certainly Christ and his truth, his gospel and its work shall overcome at the last. And overruled by him who is wonderful in counsel and excellent in working, this darkness and hindrance shall be to commend and set off the superior glory that shall yet be cast upon the people of God and the increasing work of the Lord, which shall yet appear upon the earth. And out of weakness, the shaken, trembling saints shall yet be made strong and more firmly established in the precious truths of the everlasting gospel to the glory of our great Lord and the joy of those that love him.

The Lord hath begun, my dear brethren, to give peace to the Tabernacle Society in L-------n after their great trouble to revive his work in the midst of them and to increase them since the division that hath been amongst them. And I trust the same blessings will spread over all the societies and richly distill upon your dear souls. Wherefore, "Trust ye in the Lord forever, for in the Lord Jehovah there is everlasting strength,"[2] and "they that wait for him shall not be ashamed."[3]

Great reason have you, my dear brethren, to rejoice in the Lord alway. In the Lord that hath loved you and washed you from your sins in his own blood. In the Lord that hath loved you when dead in sins and said unto you, "Live." For your present life of grace shall by him be maintained and increased until it is raised into the life of glory. Christ lives for you, lives in you, and you shall live in and with him. You that have looked to Christ for life shall be "saved in the Lord with an everlasting salvation and shall not be ashamed nor confounded, world without end!"[4] The Lord is your portion, and you are his. And what can you want or desire more? The lines are fallen unto you in pleasant places; yea, you have a goodly heritage in having Christ for your portion. And such is his infinite grace that he thus esteems of and rejoiceth in you as his.

And who or what shall separate you from his love? None of all your enemies, within nor without: neither height, nor depth, neither life, nor death, neither things present, nor things to come, shall be able to separate you from the love of God which is in Christ Jesus our Lord.[5] In the faith then, of God's free, unchangeable, everlasting love to you, walk in love to him as his dear, his obedient children. And live in love to and peace with each other. And the God of love and peace shall be with you. The grace of our Lord Jesus Christ be with your spirit!

In him, my dear brethren, I am

Your most affectionate friend and servant,

---

[2] Isaiah 26:4.
[3] Isaiah 49:23.
[4] Isaiah 45:17.
[5] Romans 8:38–39.

10
Discouragement in Gospel Ministry

LETTER XXXVI. To Mrs. P--------.

My dear sister in our precious Lord,

... O my dear sister, have you and others been driven away as it were from that rest, joy, and solace which you once enjoyed in Zion, your compassionate Jesus will seek your souls and bring you again from every place whither you have been driven in the cloudy and dark day and cause you to feed and to lie down upon the goodly mountains of Israel. While the heavenly dew, the rich distillations of the Spirit of grace, and the bright shining of the Sun of Righteousness make your pastures green, fat, and flourishing. The Lord will do better for you at your latter end than at your beginnings. ...

As to yourself, my dear sister, you need much wisdom to behave with that love and duty to Christ, with that zeal for his gospel and interest which is looked for from one of his witnesses; and yet with that humility, meekness, and patience towards those that oppose, which becomes a disciple of the meek and lowly Jesus.

But the grace of Christ is sufficient for you. Ask [for] fresh supplies daily to strengthen and guide you continually, that Christ may be glorified in you and you in him, according to the will of God and our Father.

Labour, my dear sister, to adorn the doctrine of God our Saviour by your good conversation in Christ. O covet to be a living practical proof that there is such a thing as personal holiness communicated from Christ to Christians and maintained and increased in them by him. In the Lord's strength, attempt this your duty, my dear sister. And whenever you fail, wash by faith in the Lamb's blood and be clean. And instantly set about your work again to perfect holiness in the fear of God.

O how much service would you do for our great Lord if by your holy conversation others may be convinced of the truth, which they now oppose!

Ask the prince of grace to cast this favour upon you, and in the way of your duty, wait for this mercy.

And if it should please the Lord to deny your request, if those you wish to gain should not be gathered from their strayings, yet shall you be glorious in the eyes of the Lord, and your God shall be your strength. Your work shall shortly appear to have been with the Lord and your reward with your God. When of the freest grace, he rewards his servants according to their works and according to what they would have done for him as well as according to what they actually did.

That you may walk in the comforts of the Holy Ghost and be edified is the sincere desire of, my dear sister,

Yours most affectionately in Christ,

11
Joy Amidst Hardship

LETTER XLIV. To Mrs. C---------s.

My dear sister,

How good is the Lord to us! He tries us for a while and then he comforts us. Light and darkness, joy and sorrow, bitter and sweet are wisely mixed and graciously overruled for the glory of God in our salvation. Oh, the infinite wisdom of our leader; the glory of his conduct; the happiness of those under his care; and the blissful end to which he brings them! Happy is their way, and happy is their end. Happy are they in the midst of griefs. Because the God of joy, God their joy, their exceeding joy, is with them there. Happy are they when delivered from grieving things. Because God their deliverer is their deliverance. Jesus our Redeemer, the Captain of our salvation, marches on before his redeemed, treads down the briars and thorns of the wilderness and gives us a comfortable passage through them to the land of rest.

What need we fear since the Lord is with us? With us when we pass through the waters and walk through the fires—that the one doth not consume us nor the other overflow us? Our happiness lies in having an interest in the all-sufficient God, in the enjoyment of him as such, and in our entire dedication to his glory in every changing providence. To have God in everything; to eye God in everything; and to love, bless, and adore God in everything will make everything sweet to us. And without this, nothing will be substantial, nothing joyous, nothing profitable, nothing savoury to a newborn soul as such.

Oh, what a heap of empty vanities and cruel vexations are all things which this world affords without God enjoyed, without God revered in everything! It may well be said, "To glorify God and to enjoy him is the chief end of man." And ineffably happy is that man who eagerly pursues this great end as his chief good. That man is prepared for the enjoyment, for the employment of heaven. And the more he answers that character, the greater is his preparation for the heavenly state, yea, the more of heaven comes down into his soul while his abode is on this earth.

Wishing daily fellowship with the Father, and with his Son Jesus Christ, by the Holy Ghost, the Comforter, and requesting your prayers for me, I am, my dear sister,

Yours affectionately,

PART III
A Letter to all the Saints on the General Duty of Love

"There is no case the saints can be in while in the world wherein they want so much pity and tenderness to be shown them as when wounded by sin. If therefore we would love them at all, let us be sure to do it when they most want it."

Provenance

Written and printed in London in the early forties, *A Letter to All the Saints on the General Duty of Love* was Anne Dutton's earnest exhortation to the addressed "Much honoured and beloved brethren" to practice 1 John 4:7, a verse printed on the cover of the approximately 52-page letter: "Beloved, let us love one another: for Love is of God; and every one that loveth is born of God, and knoweth God."

Dutton's autobiography reveals her thoughts while writing *Duty of Love*: she recognized her own inadequacy—for did she do *her* Christian duty to love? Her entry on November 16, 1741 shows that verses like Psalm 103:13 and Romans 14:18 reassured her: "though I was a poor, weak, imperfect creature in love, yet in as much as I desired to serve my Father herein, and to encourage his dear children so to do, he would not deal with me in the wrath of a terrible judge but have compassion on me in the bowels of a Father." Dutton was concerned about the possible condemning response from her recipients. The entry reveals that her resolve to finish the letter was stirred by her desire for the advancement of the "glory of Christ" and the "advantage" to be reaped by the saints. Dutton knew full well that she was just as needy for the counsel she was giving: "And as to teach others and not do the same things myself is an aggravated sin, so I desire to watch and that hereby I may be the more quickened to the obedience of love."[1]

The spirit in which the letter was written is revealed in its closing: "And so, my dear brethren, perhaps this may be the last work, the last service of this kind I may ever do for you, and this the last time you may hear from me. Let me therefore entreat you with my whole heart,

---

[1] Watson, *Autobiography*, 187–188.

The Spirituality of Anne Dutton

and myself also, to be followers of God, as dear children, and to walk in love as Christ also hath loved us." Dutton would live until 1765 but, frequently beset by illness, seems to have penned the letter as though it were her final one.

Her sense of urgency arose from seeing the divisiveness surfacing among Christian leaders in England.[2] Their love unmistakeable at the beginning of the Evangelical Revival, Dutton was afraid that its waning was hurting their gospel witness. Her conscientious treatment of the subject of love can be more fully appreciated when observing her grave tone in the letter's conclusion:

> Oh surely, our decay in love is one great cause of that general decay of the power of godliness which is amongst us! … If we continue in our lukewarmness, neither cold nor hot in our love to the Lord and his people, he will most certainly spew us out of his mouth. And how near that awful day is, a little more time may discover. The Lord will not always bear with our deadness since we have a name to live, but will put us into the furnace and melt us down to purge away our dross and brighten our grace.[3]

While those in the English evangelical community remained committed to foundational Christian beliefs and practices—theologically they began to hold differing views that at times led to uncharitable interactions.

This letter is therefore one of admonition as much as instruction. The blessings of God's love and salvation, beautifully witnessed early on in the revival, must be recalled: "Oh did we not enjoy a soul-satisfying sweetness, a ravishing glory in God and his service when we were first converted to him and made religion our business!"[4] Dutton reminds the letter's recipients, professors of faith in England, that this was so even "when we went after him in the wilderness in a land that was not sown, when we first set out for God and his service under the

---

[2] Dutton, *Duty of Love*, 47–48.
[3] Dutton, *Duty of Love*, 48.
[4] Dutton, *Duty of Love*, 50.

Part III: On the General Duty of Love

attracting displays of his love in the face of a thousand difficulties."[5] And more importantly, that this can and must be restored: "Oh let us therefore consider how awfully we have departed from the Lord and at his call, with weeping and with supplications, return unto him again. For he will heal our backslidings and love us freely."[6]

With such a mission in view, Dutton proceeds to methodically describe the Christian's duty of love, biblically and theologically explaining why, from where it flows, what it comprises, what its end is, why it ought not to feel like duty, how Christians have fallen short, and what their encouragement is. While the specific recipients and controversy to which Dutton refers are not revealed, the contents of this letter no doubt remain valuable and pertinent to the present-day church.[7]

---

[5] Dutton, *Duty of Love*, 49.
[6] Dutton, *Duty of Love*, 51.
[7] As indicated in the Introduction of this book, a cross-section of this letter (approximately half of it) has been presented here to allow the reader to grasp the central ideas of Dutton's exposition on the principles and practice of Christian love.

12
A Letter to All the Saints on the General Duty of Love

Much honoured and beloved brethren,

You may well wonder at my boldness in this general address. I beg leave to assure you that it is not from a sense of my ability but of duty. Nothing less than a full persuasion that it is the mind of your great Lord to send you a message by so mean a worm could have induced me to it. Humble yourselves therefore to a little child, and despise not the lispings of a babe, as the Lord of heaven and earth shall reveal his mind to it and open the babe's mouth to point out the same unto you.

Love to God and our neighbour is the sum of our duty required by the moral law, and most strongly is this enforced by the grace of the gospel. We should love God for himself, for the infinite excellencies of his great being, and for his great goodness toward us, and especially as displayed in Christ. And we should love everything else for his sake, all creatures and things, according to that relation they bear to him and the displays of his glory which is upon them. Hence, it is that the saints ought to have the chief place in our affections and especially as this is our Lord's command: "This is my commandment," says he, "that ye love one another, as I have loved you."[1] And saith the apostle John, "Beloved, if God so loved us, we ought also to love one another."[2] Love to the saints therefore being the theme I would insist on, I shall as enabled give some hints:

---

[1] John 15:12.
[2] 1 John 4:11.

I. Of the reasons and grounds why the saints should love one another.
II. Of the duty itself, or what is contained in it.
III. Of the ends of it, or what should induce us to the performance hereof. And,
IV. With a word of exhortation conclude the whole.

The reasons

I begin with the reasons and grounds why the saints should love one another.

Ground 1

The love of God to us is the great, the original ground, why we should love one another. The love of God to us in all his persons lays us under the highest obligation to love him again and one another for his sake. Are we, our individual persons, beloved of God, the Father in election? Hath he fixed his heart's love upon us, passed by others, and chosen us in his dear Son before the world was unto endless glory with him, although as considered sinners we had deserved a place in eternal torments with the devils? Oh, what obligation doth this lay us under, to love him and his! Has God the Father, of old, appointed us to obtain salvation through Jesus Christ and to be happy in time and to eternity in a love-union with himself and each other in his dear Son? And shall we be at variance among ourselves! Shall we, by want of love to each other, do all that in us lies to thwart this great end of electing love!

Are we redeemed by the Lamb's blood out of every nation, kindred, tongue, and people from endless misery to eternal glory? Oh, what obligation doth this lay us under to love the Redeemer and his redeemed! Has our dear Lord loved us and given himself for us to make us one in love among ourselves, one in him and in the Father? And shall we yet be at variance as if the Lamb was not slain! Shall we, by want of unity of affection with each other, do all in us lies to contradict the great end of his death and hereby walk as enemies to the Cross of Christ!

Part III: On the General Duty of Love

Are we the temples of the Holy Ghost? Has the Holy Spirit sent from the Father and the Son come down in his boundless love and took possession of our souls to form Christ's image, his love-image there and to bring us up to that love-unity with God and each other, which was ordained and procured for us in electing and redeeming grace? How great is our obligation hence to love the Holy Ghost and those in whom he dwells! The world hath not seen, known, nor received him. But is this our happy lot from the riches of distinguishing favour? Surely we are debtors to the Spirit! And shall we, by being at variance among ourselves, do all we can to contradict the great end of the Spirit's work!...

Ground 2

That near relation which the saints have to God and that special interest he hath in them is another ground why we should love them. They are the children of God's love, his dear children. God the Father hath predestinated them into the adoption of children by Jesus Christ unto himself. He has set them apart for himself as his own children. ... They are the choice of the Father, the purchase of the Son, and the conquest of the Spirit. The Lord hath chosen, bought, possessed them for himself as his own portion. He esteems them as his jewels, his peculiar treasure, and they are unspeakably precious and highly honourable in his sight. They are his honourable servants to do his glorious work, his faithful witnesses in the earth, and his shining lights in a dark world. ...

Ground 3

The excellency of the saints is another reason why we should love them. They are the excellent of the earth, in whom is all Christ's delight. And are they not then worthy to be ours! ... And shall not we then admire their beauty and love them exceedingly! There is none like them in the earth. They are men of another spirit from the men of the world. They are of a more noble extract, of a heavenly birth, and bound for a heavenly country, and are therefore most lovely in themselves and most worthy of love from all those who have eyes to see their glory. ...

Ground 4

That near relation which the saints have to each other is another reason why we should love them. We are all of one, children of the same Father, dear children, unspeakably dear to him who hath adopted us, unto him who hath begotten us, and should therefore walk in love. We are brethren and should therefore have brotherly kindness to each other. Since we are brethren, we should not strive, nor fall out by the way, but be one in affection as we are one in relation. Again, the saints are members of the same body, of that body whereof Christ is the head: "No man ever yet hated his own flesh, but nourisheth and cherisheth it, even as the Lord the Church."[3]…

Ground 5

That community the saints have in sufferings and in glories is a great reason why they should love one another. The same common enemies—sin, Satan, and the world—are jointly engaged against them all. … The same afflictions of this kind are accomplished in the brethren throughout the whole world. Not one of them escapes sufferings from the policy and power of hell, from the legions of devils combined against them. And as for the world of wicked men, they all hate them. Christ has chosen his people out of the world, and therefore the world hate them. He hath sent them into the world to do some work or other for him, and the world slight, despise, and reproach them, yea, were it in their power, would extirpate them out of the earth. And all these enemies—sin, Satan, and the world, even all the powers of darkness within and without—are combined together against the saints, against all of them, to overthrow their faith, to hinder their holiness, to destroy their comfort, and to prevent their usefulness in the earth, and so, their glorifying their Father in this world and their crown of glory in that to come.

And one main way in which they labour to perform their enterprises against them is this: by doing all they can to break their love to each

---

[3] Ephesians 5:29.

other. Oh then, what reason have the saints to love one another! To watch and pray and use all appointed means that brotherly love may continue! Are all the enemies of Christ and the saints combined together against them all? And do they all strive to break their love? Oh, how should the saints mutually love and sympathize with each other in their joint sufferings? And labour to unite so much the closer in love as the enemies seek to divide them! Sin is their bitter enemy. And shall they not sympathize with one another in their sufferings on this account? … Oh, shall the dear saints join issue with the powers of darkness and hate and persecute, bite and devour one another! Oh, shall we not watch, pray, and strive against this sin, this horrid sin of want of love to the saints, which is such a reproach to the Christian name! …

Ground 6

Add to all these the command of God and of the Lord Jesus Christ that we should love one another, and how great is the saint's obligation to this duty: "And this is his commandment," saith the apostle John, "That we should believe on the name of his Son Jesus Christ, and love one another as he gave us commandment. …"[4] Oh then, if we have any regard to the divine authority over us or a spark of ingenuity in our souls to the God of love, let us love one another as he hath given us commandment! …

The duty

Of the duty itself or what is contained in it. And in general, it contains
1. The inward affection of love in the heart. And,
2. The outward expression thereof all manner of ways.

For the first, we are commanded to be kindly affectioned to each other and to love one another with a pure heart fervently, in which is forbidden all disaffection, wrath, envy, hatred, and malice against our brethren. And required that we love them simply, purely, as we love

---

[4] 1 John 3:23. Dutton continues to quote John 15:17, 14:15; and 1 John 5:3.

ourselves with the same kind of love that from a dearness, a strength of affection, we interest ourselves in all their joys and sorrows, participate with them in both, and make them by sympathy, in a sort, our own.

And hence, secondly, all manner of outward unkindness to our brethren and evil entreating of them is forbidden; and all manner of outward expressions of kindness required or that we express our kindness to them all manner of ways. And who can reckon up all the ways wherein the saint should outwardly express the inward affection of their hearts to each other? But in general, they may be reduced to this: that in all things and at all times, we do to all the saints as we would they should unto us. And the pattern, the exemplar of the kindness we should show to each other is very high: that we love one another in our measure, both inwardly and outwardly, as Christ hath loved us. That we think no service too mean nor work too hard to serve our brethren in, which the Lord hath commanded.

… there are four channels especially in which this love should run.

Compassion towards our brethren in their sins and sufferings

We should consider our brethren as being ourselves also in the body, liable to sins and sorrows, and not be angry with them when they have sinned; no, not, though they have sinned against us. We may be angry with sin, but not with our sinning brother. We ought to love his person while angry with his sin: "If we would be angry and 'sin not,' we must (as a dear deceased servant of Christ once observed) be angry with nothing but sin."

Sin is indeed the most hateful evil, and our brethren have this hateful evil abiding in them, and through the subtlety of Satan and the snares of the world, they are liable to fall into sin many ways. And when they have so done, let us by love and sympathy make their case our own and behave towards them as we would be glad to have them do towards us were they in our case and we in theirs. Let us consider that their sins are their sufferings, their soul-sicknesses, and heart-wounds, and commiserate them accordingly. And let our pity towards them be shown in

Part III: On the General Duty of Love

endeavouring to restore them in the spirit of meekness; let us set their broken bones with all possible tenderness. ...[5]

And yet, in appearing against our brother's sin, let us do it with all meekness, wisdom, and faithfulness, and with all the privacy the case will bear according to the rules our Lord has given us in his Word. If our brother's fault be private, let us not make it public and thereby wound the public honour of Jesus Christ and uncover our brother's nakedness. ...

When any of our brethren are fallen therefore, let us not triumph over them, despise, insult, and upbraid them with their faults. Let us not have high thoughts of ourselves as if we were better than they. The case might have been, and perhaps, as bad or worse may be our own. No reason have we to be high-minded but to fear. And let us be as careful to cover our brother's infirmities as to hide our own. Christ covers innumerable faults in us with the mantle of his love and brings us to a sense of our evil in private between him and us alone. ...

And as soon as the Lord gives repentance and manifests pardon unto any of our sinning brethren, let us from the heart forgive them too, confirm our love towards them, and mention their faults no more, even as Christ and God for his sake hath forgiven us and remembers our sins no more.[6] And though our brethren should often offend and grieve us, yet should we bear with and exercise all long-suffering towards them, considering how much the Lord bears with in us daily and that infinite patience and long-suffering, which he exerciseth towards us under all our repeated provocations. ...

There is no case the saints can be in while in the world wherein they want so much pity and tenderness to be shown them as when wounded by sin. If therefore we would love them at all, let us be sure to do it when they most want it. ...

---

[5] Galatians 6:1.
[6] 2 Corinthians 2:7; Ephesians 4:32.

Forbearance towards them in their present imperfect state

We don't all yet see eye to eye. There are different measures of faith and light distributed among the saints by the sovereign Lord of all, both with respect to the doctrine of the gospel and the discipline of the church. And through the corruption of our nature, there is an aptness to slight and despise, yea to speak evil of our brethren that are not just of our length and breadth. This is contrary to love.

If we love our brethren as we ought, we shall love them for Christ's sake because they belong to Christ, and not merely, first or principally, because they are of the same way of thinking with us. The way to heaven is indeed strait, yet is there some latitude in it. The saints, as strangers and pilgrims on earth, are all travelling home to their Father's house in heaven, in Christ the strait way. Yet some walk in Christ in one path of duty, and some in another according to the proportion of faith given them.

And though we don't all walk in the same path, yet shall we all meet at last: Christ the way will bring us all to the Father. And shall we not then love as brethren! If we can't walk together in all things as to externals, let us walk in love, even all that are Christ's, in the very inward affection of our souls to each other. So far as we can discern any to hold the head Christ, of which we ourselves are members, let us be one in love with them. …

But here I would not be mistaken as if I thought that any of the truths of Christ either as to doctrine or discipline were little in themselves and not much to be regarded by us. Nor that we ought not to contend earnestly for the faith once delivered to the saints. Nor yet that we ought not to obey the truth so far as we know it. No. Truth, every part of it, is precious. We ought to buy it and sell it not, to put a value upon it according to its own worth and not to part with a jot of it. And so far as we discern the truth, we ought to be living witnesses thereof in the earth. And by no means ought we to imprison or disobey the truth by yielding to any error, either in doctrine or discipline, contrary to the light of our own consciences. For these things are a main part of our generation-work in the earth. …

Part III: On the General Duty of Love

Nor yet do I think that we may not lawfully have a greater complacency in those saints which walk more eminently in the truth than others. Doubtless there is a peculiar sweetness attends communion where brethren are agreed in judgment, and unity in judgment tends to make unity of affection more strong. And justly ought to do so, so far as our brethren walk with us in the truth. That is, we ought to love them as holding the truth, not for our own sakes because they hold the same truths that we do, but for the truth's sake that dwelleth in them and us. But then our love to the brethren ought not to be confined to those only that are agreed with us in judgment, but to extend itself to all, even to those which differ the most from us. We are not to love their imperfections, darkness, errors, but ought to love their persons under them. To love them as brethren, to love them for Christ's sake as they are his servants, his children, and members of his body....

Earnest endeavours after their happiness and glory
If we love them, we should seek their good. It is the nature of love not to seek its own but the good and happiness of the object beloved. The saints are beloved of God and appointed to happiness and glory, and therefore we ought to love them and seek these for them. And the happiness and glory of the saints relate:
1. To their persons.
2. To their work. And,
3. To their reward.

Their happiness and glory with respect to their persons consists in their holiness and joy, the increase and abundance of both. With respect to their work, in their assistance for it and success in it. And with respect to their reward, in that abundant peace, which like a river is extended to them here, and that praise, honour, and glory, which shall be conferred upon them in the day of Christ.

All which we are to seek for the saints most earnestly, whether considered distinctly or jointly, as particular believers or united bodies in church fellowship. We are to say concerning them in both respect,

"Peace be within thy walls, and prosperity within thy palaces. For my brethren and companions' sakes; because of the house of the Lord our God, I will seek thy good."[7]

... If we loved our brethren, how ready should we be to help and serve them in their outward wants! If we loved them, how ready should we be to impart spiritual gifts to them! Oh that ever there should be any wretched selfishness in our souls, any carelessness about our brethren's welfare! If therefore we love Christ and them, let us earnestly seek their happiness and glory. And in order hereto, let us not be strangers to each other as little as possible. Let us acquaint ourselves with the saints, get knowledge of their cases, make them our own, carry them to the Lord, and afford all the help to them we are capable of.

Visiting the saints is one of the duties of love we owe them. They that fear the Lord should speak often one to another. And I have experienced a very great blessing to attend it unto mutual edification in love. 'Tis a part of the communion of saints. And let us not make excuses that we haven't time. Short visits well improved are far preferable to long ones misimproved. If we would have our visits spiritual to turn to some account to the glory of God, the good of our brethren, and to our own advantage, let us first seek God that he would go with us to his dear children. And when we come to them, let us instantly begin with spiritual converse to know the state of their souls. And watch that the whole of our discourse be spiritual and pertinent, that we don't step out for a moment into needless, vain conversation.

And when we return, let us spread all before the Lord, give thanks, and pray for them as the case requires, and supplicate the throne for a blessing to rest upon them and us in that labour of love we have been enabled to perform towards them. And when we know their cases, let us keep them as private as we do our own and only use our interest with God for them and labour to speak a word in season to them. It is the glory of a Christian to be like Christ, and the more likeness to him we attain, the more room will there be in our hearts for the cases of his

---

[7] Psalm 122:7–9.

Part III: On the General Duty of Love

children. If we loved them with a pure heart fervently, we should have an ear open to all their complaints and a bosom large enough to receive all their griefs, their sorrows, and their joys—and be sensibly touched with both as we got knowledge thereof in visiting them. Oh, were such visits mutually, frequently, and conscientiously kept up among the saints, how much would they promote heart-unity and brotherly love among them! …

And in a word, let us do all we can, all manner of ways, to nourish and cherish them and to encourage them in the way and work of the Lord—in the closet, family, and church—that their holiness may increase and their usefulness be abundant; that their happiness may be great in this world and their glory in that to come. …

Rejoicing with them in all their joy

For this is a channel in which our love towards them should flow. As we should weep with them that weep, so likewise rejoice with them that rejoice. If one member is honoured, the rest should rejoice with it.[8] If our brethren increase in grace, gifts, honour, and usefulness, we love them not if we don't rejoice with them. And in this duty of love, in rejoicing with them, as all envy and evil-speaking against them is forbidden, so all joy in the inward affection and outward expressions thereof commanded.

We ought in no wise to grudge at and envy our brethren when they rise in grace, gifts, and usefulness, in honour and esteem; no, though they be near us, and we may imagine that our own is somewhat eclipsed thereby. Oh, what wretched selfishness is it when we are afraid our brethren should outshine us and therefore slight them in our hearts and speak lightly or perhaps reproachfully of them to others and tell their faults to eclipse their virtues that we might rise by their ruin! …

That it is meet[9] our God should display his glories in, upon, and by all his saints, and that he is worthy to be loved, admired, and glorified

---

[8] Romans 12:15; 1 Corinthians 12:26.
[9] Meaning, "Fit; proper; qualified." Johnson, Samuel. "Meet." *A Dictionary of the English Language*, https://johnsonsdictionaryonline.com/1755/meet_adj, 1755. Accessed June 20, 2023.

by us in them all. That it is meet our brethren should quietly possess all that happiness and joy which free grace bestows upon them. And that they by shining in their own sphere will not hinder our brightness. Oh, shall we limit an infinite being and desire his manifestative glories to be confined to ourselves? Shall we think our brethren unworthy of that glory which God has thought them worthy of? And that their brightness will eclipse ours? No, far be such a spirit from us!

The God of our Lord Jesus Christ, the Father of glory, hath laid out the exceeding riches of his grace in allotting the saints their several orbs, their several spheres of action and glories with which they shine in the church-heaven. And one by performing his own duty and shining in his own glory don't hinder another in what properly belongs to him any more than the stars of heaven in their different orbs obstruct each other's motion or obscure each other's brightness, or than the angels of light in their different orders and several employments interfere with each other's service or glory. ...

Hence then, if we love God and his glory, our brethren and their happiness, yea, ourselves and our own bliss, let us rejoice with the saints in all their joy. For the glory of God is advanced by all the honour he confers upon his children and all the joy he gives them. And the happiness of our brethren consists therein. And as our own personal bliss is full in our own place, so our relative bliss rises with the advance of our brethren's. The members of Christ's body have each their own part of happiness and glory, full and entire, which none can rob them of, yet have they it not separately by and for themselves alone but with and for the rest. The glory put upon each member advanceth the body's glory, and the glory of the whole body devolves upon every member by reason of that unity of life and community of bliss which is between them. ...

O then, let us that are members of Christ's body in the unity of the Spirit have but one joy! And in that one joy mutually rejoice with and over each other to possess that one glory, which flows and reflows through and upon the whole! And from the inward affection of joy in our hearts, let the outward expressions thereof flow. In mutual rejoicings before God and giving thanks unto him for one another's bliss.

Part III: On the General Duty of Love

And in congratulations of each other, both privately and publicly, as the case requires, while the blessings of heaven in free favours unto full joys descend upon the heirs of God! ...

The ends
Of the ends of it, or what should induce us to the performance hereof. And these are,
1. The glorifying of God in all his persons.
2. The comfort and edification of our brethren.
3. The conviction of wicked men. And
4. Our own peace, joy, and holiness here, and our Lord's approbation of us at his appearing.

The glorifying of God
The pleasing and glorifying of God in all his persons is a special end why we should love the saints. The glory of God ought to be the chief end of all our actions in general, and so of the performance of this duty, of love to the saints in particular.

"Herein is my Father glorified," says our Lord, "that ye bring forth much fruit,"[10] and the fruit that is especially intended here is love:[11] "This is my commandment, that ye love one another." And says the apostle, "Be ye therefore followers of God, as dear children."[12] The God and Father of our Lord Jesus Christ and our God and Father in him is glorified hereby when we walk in love to each other. It is his will that his love to us in the image thereof in us should stand forth to be beheld by others in our love to our brethren.

That we should show what dear children we are to him and what an influence his dear love to us hath upon our souls by the dearness of our love to each other. And as he hath given us commandment that we should love one another as he hath loved us, we ought to do it, that we may glorify him, both in his love to us and authority over us. We ought

---
[10] John 15:8.
[11] John 15:12.
[12] Ephesians 5:1.

likewise to do this that we may please him. When we walk in love as dear children, it is highly pleasing to our Father: "And as ye have received of us how ye ought to walk," says the apostle, "and to please God, see that ye abound more and more."[13]...

The comfort of the saints

The comfort and edification of the saints is a great end why we should love them. Love brings abundance of comfort to the saints in all the times that pass over them, in prosperity and adversity. It easeth them when oppressed, enlightens them when dark, warms them when cold, revives them when fainting, strengthens them when weak, heals them when diseased, and enlargeth them when in confinement; and when rejoicing, it makes their joy more full.

It sweetens all their bitter potions and makes their pleasant things more delicious. And in a word, it is as it were a stream of heaven's joy and sweetness let out upon their souls, which wafts them apace towards that ocean of joy and glory which is there prepared for them. And as there is much comfort of love, so much edification. "Knowledge puffeth up, but charity edifieth."[14] It builds up saints and churches and raiseth them apace to be a habitation of God through the Spirit....

The conviction of the wicked

The conviction of wicked men is another end why the saints should love one another. "By this shall all men know that ye are my disciples," saith our Lord, "if ye have love one to another."[15] Love is a main duty whereby we should put to silence the ignorance of foolish men. If we loved the brotherhood as we ought, if we were one pure piece of love to each other, what a conviction would this strike into the consciences of the wicked!

Love is of God and by this the children of God are manifest. Wherever love is to be seen in the saints towards each other and to all men,

---

[13] 1 Thessalonians 4:1.
[14] Philippians 2:1; 1 Corinthians 8:1.
[15] John 13:35.

Part III: On the General Duty of Love

it shines with a convincing glory that God dwells in such persons and that they are of God. The wicked can't see the saints in their inward heart-glory, but they see their outward carriage. And when this is contrary to love, it hardens them in their sin, gives them occasion to blaspheme that worthy name by which we are called and makes them think that there's nothing in religion. And indeed, if we hate, bite, and devour one another, it makes us look very unlike the disciples of our meek and loving master, Christ; and ill becomes our character as the sheep of his pasture, the doves of his delight.

If therefore we would commend the ways of God to others and strike sinners with a conviction of their excellency and glory, let us walk in love. …

Our peace, joy, and holiness

If we regard our own peace, joy, and holiness here, and our Lord's approbation of us at his appearing, let us love one another with a pure heart fervently.

We cannot make war against our brethren, but we break our own peace. As hereby we dishonour and displease the God of love and peace, and grieve the sacred dove, so he leaves us to our own spirits to be like a troubled sea, which cannot rest, whose waters cast up mire and dirt. Whereas if we walk in love, we have great peace, abundant peace, though war should be round about us. If our brethren don't love us as they ought, yet if we love them and render love for unkindness and blessing for cursing, we have abundant peace, peace like a river overflowing our souls. "Great peace have they that love God's law; his law of love, and nothing shall offend them."[16]

And so far as we are lacking in our love to the saints, so far our joy is imperfect. In keeping Christ's command of loving one another as he hath loved us, our joy is full. This was his end in giving it and ought to be ours in obeying it.[17] And so much as we are wanting in love to the saints, so much we are wanting in holiness. Love is as it were the very

---

[16] Psalm 119:165.
[17] John 14:11.

essence of a Christian, of Christianity in his soul. As appears from 1 Corinthians 13: whatever we are in other gifts and duties, without love, we are nothing in true Christianity, we are nothing in real holiness. So far as we love God and each other, just so much is our holiness; as the one increaseth, the other advanceth. Love is a perfecting grace, and, as our great duty, is our great privilege. So much as we love one another, so much we are like God, and so much fruit we bring forth. So far as our love abounds, our meetness for glory increaseth.

And therefore the apostle prayed for the Thessalonians that "the Lord would make them to increase and abound in love one towards another and to all men. To the end he might establish their hearts unblameable in holiness before him."[18] And we ought to increase and abound in love to each other unto unblameable holiness before God, with an eye to that great day when our Lord shall appear as it follows: at the coming of our Lord Jesus Christ with all his saints. …

"For we must all appear before the judgment seat of Christ, that every one may receive the things done in his body (in praise or rebuke, in glory or shame) according to that he hath done, whether it be good or bad.[19] If therefore we would have our Lord's well done, his approbation of us as good and faithful servants, as obedient children at his coming, let us show all brotherly kindness to each other in love. For not the least favour we ever showed to the least of his shall be lost in that day. Our Lord will then commend our obedience before all and declare how kindly he took it, even as done to himself. And so an entrance shall be ministered unto us abundantly into his everlasting kingdom.[20]

Conclusion

I shall, with a word of exhortation, conclude the whole. …

Oh, who of us can say we are clean from this abomination of inordinate self-love and want of love to our brethren! …

---

[18] 1 Thessalonians 3:12–13.
[19] 2 Corinthians 5:9–10.
[20] Matthew 25:40; 2 Peter 1:11.

Part III: On the General Duty of Love

Oh surely our decay in love is one great cause of that general decay of the power of godliness which is amongst us! Or rather, it is the thing itself! We have left God and provoked him to depart from us, and he is gone in a great measure as to his sensible, powerful presence from the persons, families, and churches of the saints. His glory seems to be upon the threshold of the house. And unless we remember from whence we are fallen, repent, and do our first works, he will quite forsake us, remove our candlestick out of its place, and give up the dearly beloved of his soul into the hand of her enemies. ...

Oh did we not enjoy a soul-satisfying sweetness, a ravishing glory in God and his service when we were first converted to him and made religion our business! Wherefore then do we say, "We are Lords, we will come no more at him!" Why are we careless about his service, the obedience of love, as if we were our own! And contented to live at such a distance from communion with God in love and conformity to him as the most of us do at this day! Oh, is not our God and his service our glory! And can we forget him—our adorning, our bright array—and walk naked as it were before men, unclothed of those glories we once shone in!

And yet this is the case. We have forgotten our God, days without number! We have changed our glory for that which doth not profit but is matter of our shame! Yet hath not our God forgotten us? No. "Go," saith he, "and proclaim these words toward the north, and say, Return thou backsliding Israel, saith the Lord, and I will not cause mine anger to fall upon you, for I am merciful, saith the Lord, and I will not keep anger forever. Only acknowledge thine iniquity that thou hast transgressed against the Lord thy God and hast scattered thy ways unto the strangers under every green tree, and ye have not obeyed my voice, saith the Lord."[21] Oh, let us therefore consider how awfully we have departed from the Lord, and at his call, with weeping and with supplications, return unto him again. For he will heal our backslidings and

---

[21] Jeremiah 3:12–13.

love us freely. And this will make us love him and one another fervently.

And after this fervent love, let us earnestly seek; that from henceforth, in deed and in truth, we may love as brethren. Let brotherly love continue. And in a due use of all appointed means, let us labour to increase therein more and more. Aye, even those of us that are the warmest in love, let us supplicate the throne, that the Spirit of love may be poured down upon us. Let us keep ourselves in the love of God, abide in Christ by faith, and keep his words in love; and so the Father will love us, and the Son will love us, and both will come and make their abode with us. And by their presence with us in love, in manifestative love, our souls will be changed into the same image from glory to glory and sweetly disposed to love our brethren.

And let us labour all manner of ways to keep them also under the sweet influence of God's love, that their hearts, under the transforming shine of love's glory, may likewise be disposed to love us. That while the bright beams of eternal love cast their glories upon us all, we may mutually reflect the same upon each other. That so the church militant in its love-unity may bear some resemblance of the church triumphant, our Lord's kingdom come, his will be done, and his glory advanced through all the earth.

When our Lord was about to leave his disciples, then it was he gave them this commandment to love one another. And it was in the last days of the apostle John that he said unto the saints, "Little children, let us love one another." And so, my dear brethren, perhaps this may be the last work, the last service of this kind I may ever do for you, and this the last time you may hear from me. Let me therefore entreat you with my whole heart, and myself also, to be followers of God, as dear children, and to walk in love as Christ also hath loved us. That the name of our Lord may be glorified in us, and we in him according to the will of God and our Father.

Wishing a rich unction from the holy one unto a rich increase of all grace unto all glory, and requesting your prayers for the least of Christ's, and a blessing upon this weak labour of love, I am,

Part III: On the General Duty of Love

Honoured Brethren,
Humbly and Affectionately yours,
in our dear Lord Jesus,

Acknowledgements

I would like to express my sincere gratitude to Dr. Michael Haykin for giving me yet another opportunity to immerse in a meaningful writing project. I am grateful for his vision, guidance, enabling, and encouragement. The time I have spent over the years researching and writing about women in church history have been profoundly edifying, and I count it a privilege to be granted the precious task of presenting their lives to readers.

I am incredibly grateful to Anne Dutton herself and her spiritual letters. The invitation to contribute to this project came at a time when I was personally plodding in my own wilderness, and this godly woman's gospel-saturated counsel ministered to my soul. Transcribing over 500 pages of her letters (from which I made selections) could feel monotonous at times, yet the act of typing Dutton's words kept my mind and heart marinating in God's truths and promises.

I would like to extend my thanks to Michael D. Sciretti for his Ph.D. dissertation on Dutton's spiritual direction ministry, which was a valuable resource for providing context for Dutton's letters.

Thanks also to JoAnn Ford Watson for compiling six volumes of Dutton's spiritual writings. I relied on volume 3, Dutton's autobiography, to unearth themes in Dutton's life: a physical book enabled me to easily leaf through backwards and forwards Dutton's account of her life and fill the pages with my own annotations.

A heartfelt thanks to my sister Grace Chan for reading my published works with such love and engagement. To discover at which points she is deeply encouraged—or cries—infuses in me further inspiration for this writing journey. In my writing space hangs a heartening birthday note from her from two years ago: "I love that after hours and hours, days, weeks, years of hard work, you snap a photo of a book you've written as if it just appeared. No complaining. No grumbling. You do what God leads you to do and you see the long game."

A thanks as well to my pastor, Joshua Tong, who, even with so much on his plate, readily makes the time to read the excerpts of writing I send him and replies with uplifting comments. Thanks also to my family and friends for their support and for those who have responded to my sporadic messages of Anne Dutton quotes with appreciation and anticipation of this book.

Finally, to my husband Lee I express my deepest gratitude, who has not only supported me from day one but who also manages our household so smoothly that I can regularly enter into my writer's world for hours at a time. The materialization of this book would not have been possible without him by my side.

Priscilla Wong
Richmond Hill, Ontario
June 2023

About the Author

Priscilla Wong has a degree in English literature and French from York University and a Master of Theological Studies degree from Toronto Baptist Seminary. She also received a diploma in Radio and Television Broadcasting (with a specialization in broadcast journalism) from Seneca College and a certificate in Creative Writing from the University of Toronto. Professionally, she has worked as an English tutor, technical writer, copywriter, and intern news reporter. In addition to an essay on the Pilgrim women published in H&E's *Strangers and Pilgrims on the Earth: Remembering the Mayflower Pilgrims, 1620–2020*, Priscilla is the author of *Anne Steele and her Spiritual Vision: Seeing God in the Peaks, Valleys and Plateaus of Life* (Reformation Heritage Books, 2012) and *The Bold Evangelist: The Life and Ministry of Selina Hastings, Countess of Huntingdon* (H&E Publishing, 2021). Priscilla lives in Richmond Hill, Ontario, with her husband Lee, and her three children Nathaniel, Jenuine, and Josiah. They are members of Sovereign Grace Church where Priscilla and her husband host a small group and Priscilla serves as a deacon on the children's ministry team. At present, she is balancing homeschooling with writing and teaching. Priscilla counts herself immeasurably blessed to be able to devote her time to her beloved aspirations.

Works Cited

Bebbington, David, and David Ceri Jones's. *Evangelicalism and Dissent in Modern England and Wales*. Abingdon, Oxon: Routledge, 2021.

Burder, Samuel. *Memoirs of Eminently Pious Women, Volume 2*. London: J. Duncan, Longman, 1827.

Dutton, Anne. *A Discourse upon Walking with God: In a Letter to a Friend…* London: Printed for the author and sold by E. Gardner, 1735.

_____. *A Letter to All the Saints on the General Duty of Love: Humbly Presented, by One That is Less Than the Least of Them All, and Unworthy to be of Their Happy Number*. London: Printed by John Hart and sold by J. Lewis and E. Gardner, 1743.

_____. *Letters on Spiritual Subjects, and Divers Occasions; Sent to Relations and Friends*. London: J. Hart, 1747.

_____. *Three Letters on 1. The Marks of a Child of God. II. The Soul-Diseases of God's Children; …III. God's Prohibition of His People's Unbelieving Fear: …By One Who Has Tasted that the Lord is Gracious*. London: Printed by J. Hart, in Popping's-Court, Fleet-Street, 1761.

Gordon, James M. *Evangelical Spirituality*. Eugene, Oregon: Wipf & Stock Publishers, 1991.

Haykin, Michael A.G. "English Calvinistic Baptists and Vocation in the Long Eighteenth Century, with Particular Reference to Anne Dutton's Calling as an Author." *The Southern Baptist Journal of Theology* 22:1 (Spring 2018).

_____.. "A Cloud of Witnesses." *Evangelical Times,* April 2001, accessed June 2022, https://www.evangelical-times.org/articles/historical/a-cloud-of-witnesses-21/.

Hindmarsh, D. Bruce. *The Evangelical Conversion Narrative: Spiritual Autobiography in Early Modern England*. Oxford: Oxford University, 2005.

Johnson, Samuel. *A Dictionary of the English Language*. 1755, 1773. Edited by Beth Rapp Young, Jack Lynch, William Dorner, Amy Larner Giroux, Carmen Faye Mathes, and Abigail Moreshead. 2021. https://johnsonsdictionaryonline.com

Jones, John Andrews. Preface of Anne Dutton's *A Narration of the Wonders of Grace, In Six Parts*. London: W.M. Knight and Co., 1833.

Mursell, Gordon. *English Spirituality: From 1700 to the Present Day*. London: SPCK, 2001.

Packer, J.I. *A Quest for Godliness: The Puritan Vision of the Christian Life*. Wheaton, Illinois: Crossway Books, 1990.

Sciretti, Michael D. "Anne Dutton as a Spiritual Director." *The Center for Christian Ethics at Baylor University*, 30–36 (2009), https://www.baylor.edu/content/services/docment.php/98763.pdf.

———. "'Feed My Lambs': The Spiritual Direction Ministry of Calvinistic British Baptist Anne Dutton During the Early Years of Evangelical Revival." PhD diss., Baylor University, 2009.

Stein, Stephen J. "A Note on Anne Dutton, Eighteenth-Century Evangelical." *American Society of Church History* vol. 44, no. 4 (Dec. 1975): 485–491. https://www.jstor.org/stable/3163827.

Watson, JoAnn Ford. "Anne Dutton: An Eighteenth Century British Evangelical Woman Writer." Ashland Theological Journal 30 (1998): 51–56.

Watson, JoAnn Ford. *Selected Spiritual Writings of Anne Dutton: Eighteenth-century, British-Baptist, Theologian: Volume 1: Letters*. Macon, Georgia: Mercer University, 2003.

———. *Selected Spiritual Writings of Anne Dutton: Eighteenth-century, British-Baptist, Theologian: Volume 2: Discourses, Poetry, Hymns, Memoir*. Macon, Georgia: Mercer University, 2004.

———. *Selected Spiritual Writing of Anne Dutton, Eighteenth-Century British-Baptist, Woman Theologian: Volume 3: Autobiography*. Macon, Georgia: Mercer University, 2006.

———. *Selected Spiritual Writings of Anne Dutton Eighteenth-century British-Baptist, Woman Theologian: Volume 6, Various Works*. Macon, Georgia: Mercer University, 2010.

Textual Notes and Emendations

The letters in this collection have been carefully edited to provide a more accessible read. The original unrevised version includes lengthy paragraphs; periodic sentences (in which the main point appears at the end of a very long sentence); unfamiliar punctuation usage; peculiar spelling (in addition to the "f" letter frequently being used in place of the "s"); and seemingly random capitalization and italicization of words. Editorial changes thus involved addressing these areas yet striving to remain faithful to the author's original style and intended impact. In addition, all of the spiritual letters of Anne Dutton have been emended where any of the following circumstances apply:

- Where Bible verse references appear within sentences, they have been footnoted (unless the reference is incorporated into Dutton's own sentence)

- Where past tense forms of verbs are spelled with a "y'd" or "'d" or "t" ending, they have been changed to the regular "ed" ending

- Where hyphenated words are not hyphenated in modern usage

- Where "&c." for "et cetera" appears and does not add meaning to the text, it has been removed

- Where clear discernible errors have occurred in the original text, corrections have been made

In addition, the following have been regularized throughout Dutton's letters:

- "'em" for "them"
- "thro'" for "through"
- "'twas" for "it was"
- "throughly" for "thoroughly"
- "an" for "a" where it occurs before a noun beginning with a consonant, including words where the "h" is not silent in modern speech (e.g., "an husband" for "a husband," "an hand" for "a hand," "an holy" for "a holy")
- "any where" for "anywhere"
- "every thing" for "everything"
- "for ever" for "forever"
- "mean while" for "meanwhile"
- "divers" for "diverse"
- "rejoyce" for "rejoice," "rejoycing" for "rejoicing," and "rejoyceth" for "rejoiceth"
- "ho'iness" for "holiness"
- "compleat" for "complete" and "compleatly" for "completely"
- "builded' for "built"
- "publick" for "public"
- "shew" for "show," "shewed" or "shewn" for "shown," and "shewing" for "showing"
- "cloathed" for "clothed" and "uncloath'd" for "unclothed"
- "subtilty" for "subtlety"
- "han't" for "haven't"
- "intreat" for "entreat" and "intreated" for "entreated"
- "apostolick" for "apostolic"
- "sceptre" for "scepter"
- "Sion" for "Zion"
- "stablish" for "establish"

Part III: On the General Duty of Love

- "Spue" for "spew"

Scripture Index

OLD TESTAMENT

Genesis
  22:17 50
  33:10 50
Exodus
  3:14 49
  20:3 48
  25:22 66
Leviticus
  19:17 97
Deuteronomy
  10:12–13 70
  18:15 48
  28:5–6 50
  31:6 82
  33:16 90
1 Samuel
  15:22 21
1 Chronicles
  29:14 50
2 Chronicles
  6:18 49
  15:17 62
  16:12 62
Ezra
  9:13 52
Nehemiah
  9:5 .... 16, 49, 68

Job
  4:19 49
  7:17 42
  8:9 43
  9:21 61
  13:15 .... 48, 63
  15:16 42
  16:9 61
  21:14 40
  23:10 53
  32:7 39
  33:16 52
  35:7 68
  38:2 40
  40:4 57
Psalm
  8:4 42
  8:4 64
  9:18 54
  17:14 50
  22:8 54
  24:8 44
  25:10 .... 51, 54
  30:5 54
  31:2 49
  34:8 50
  34:19 54
  37:16 50
  37:23 65
  39:9 52

45:11	46	3:9	51
47:5	44	3:17	56
49:6	50	4:18	47
51:12	59	12:28	60
55:22	54	13:20	65
67:6	51	14:10	53
68:17–18	44	15:19	60
73:23	59	16:8	50
73:25–26	42	18:10	60

Ecclesiastes

73:28	70
78:53	60

11:7	59

Song of Solomon

80:33	45	2:16	21
84:7	63	6:6	64
85:10	45	7:1	65

Isaiah

89:30	51	24:15	52
94:12	52	26:4	106
97:2	59	26:10	50
103:13	51, 113	26:13	42
107:8	50	26:19	78
113:6	16, 49	27:9	52
118:23	71	28:21	54
119	55	38:14	49
119:6	62	40:17	49
119:67	52	40:30	59
119:71	54	40:31	81
119:75	51	41:10	81
119:111	56	41:14	81
122:7–9	126	42:21	41, 45
125:2	59	43:2	51
130:3	62	43:10	52
130:4	62	43:25	99
132:13	57	45:17	106
145:1	67	48:17	55
147:1	70	49:23	106
149:9	71	50:10	48
165	132	53:4	51

Proverbs

1:14	68	53:5	41
1:32	50		

Scripture Index

54:8 45
55:7 .... 41, 45
57:14 60
57:15 .... 43, 49
57:16 54
61:10 46
62:5 57
62:5 .... 64, 65
63:9 53
64:6 61

Jeremiah
1:6 39
2:2 63
3:12–13 134
9:24 54
23:28 18
31:3 .... 40, 41, 57
31:14 .... 45, 89
31:20 54
32:41 54

Lamentations
1:16 59
3:18 20
3:29 52
3:33 54

Ezekiel
8:6 60
16:61 64
20:43 .... 61, 67

Daniel
3:25 53
9:24 45
10:19 79

Hosea
11:4 42
14:8 42

Amos
3:3 40

Micah
6:4 20
7:18 45

Nahum
1:2 40
1:3 51

Habakkuk
2:2 60
3:19 47

Zephaniah
3:12 49
3:17 42

Zechariah
4:7 67
12:10 42
13:7 43

Malachi
2:2 50
3:3 52
3:6 57
3:16 95
3:17 96

NEW TESTAMENT

Matthew
- 4:10 48
- 5:5 49
- 5:17 44
- 5:48 56
- 11:19 52
- 11:25 47
- 11:30 56
- 13:13 47
- 13:16 47
- 17:4 70
- 22:36–40 28
- 25:23 82
- 25:35 63
- 25:37 63
- 25:40 133
- 27:46 44

Luke
- 5:8 64
- 15:19 67
- 22:53 44
- 24:13–16 59
- 24:32 68

John
- 1:7 43
- 1:9, ... 43
- 1:16 46
- 3:16 41
- 3:33 47
- 6:37 100
- 7:18 69
- 8:32 68
- 8:50 69
- 11:4 52
- 13:10 64
- 13:35 131
- 14:6 43
- 14:11 132
- 14:15 66
- 14:16 ..... 59, 65
- 14:19 58
- 14:22 ..... 47, 66
- 14:23 66
- 15:7 66
- 15:8 ..... 70, 129
- 15:9 66
- 1514 66
- 15:12 ..... 117, 129
- 15:14 ..... 46, 65
- 15:15 67
- 16:14 61
- 16:14–15 66
- 17:23 41
- 20:17 45
- 20:28 99
- 21:15–16 36

Acts
- 7:2 68
- 7:59 78
- 9:31 65
- 10:36 41
- 13:48 41
- 14:22 51
- 18:26 ..... 20, 46
- 20:24 53

Romans
- 1:30 40
- 3:26 45
- 3:5 40
- 4:13 49
- 4:16 60
- 4:21 48
- 4:25 44
- 5:10 ..... 40, 58
- 5:18 44

Scripture Index

5:2 67
5:3 52
5:3–4 52
5:6 44
7:4 70
7:9 41
8:17 51
8:28 .... 46, 52
8:29 .... 41, 51
8:35 53
8:37 53
8:38–39 106
8:39 66
8:6 70
9:5 57
10:4 44
11:33 .... 51, 59
12:12 52
12:15 127
14:18 113
14:8 56
16:26 47

1 Corinthians
1:27–28 57
1:28 21
2:10 47
3:21–22 49
6:19 56
7:24 56
8:1 130
10:30–31 51
10:31 .... 56, 70
12:26 127
13:11 65

2 Corinthians
1:20 43
2:7 123
4:3 68
4:6 69

4:17 52
5:4 67
5:7 65
5:9–10 132
5:14 56
6:10 50
6:16 49
6:18 65
7:4 52
12:9 67
13–14 66

Galatians
1:16 41
3:10 40
3:13 44
4:6, ... 41
5:22 47
6:1 123

Ephesians
1:6 69
1:8 46
1:11 52
2:1 41
2:4–5 41
2:7 69
2:10 41
2:12 40
2:16 41
2:22 48
3:8 39
3:9 68
3:17 26
4:9 44
4:10 44
4:30 46
4:32 123
5:1 .... 46, 51, 129
5:29 120
6:15 65

Philippians
  1:11 69
  1:29 51
  2:1 130
  2:10–11 69
  3:3 61
  3:8–9 61
  3:12 39
  4:9 51
Colossians
  1:15 69
  1:18 44
  1:19 60
  1:20 45
  1:22 45
  1:24 51
  2:6 47
  2:15 45
  3:11 61
1 Thessalonians
  3:12–13 132
  4:1 130
  5:18 51
2 Thessalonians
  3:5 66
1 Timothy
  1:15 60
  3:16 71
  4:8 49
  6:17 51
2 Timothy
  2:19 40
  3:16–17 48
Hebrews
  1:2 48
  1:3 44
  2:11 46
  2:16 44
  3:6 48
  5:12 39
  5:14 39
  6:17 49
  6:18 47
  9:12 .... 44, 57
  9:24 .... 44, 58
  10:14 57
  10:19 46
  11:6 68
  11:11 48
  12:2 47
  12:10 52
  13:8 57
James
  2:23 65
  4:10 52
1 Peter
  1:5 46
  1:6 54
  1:6–7 52
  1:9 70
  1:12 64
  1:15 55
  1:16 56
  2:24 44
  2:5 .... 46, 56
  2:7 60
  4:11 70
  5:4 79
2 Peter
  1:11 133
1 John
  1:5 .... 7, 55
  1:7 .... 46, 62
  1:9 45
  2:1 58
  3:23 121
  4:11 117
  4:19 41

Scripture Index

4:7 113
5:7 66
Revelation
  1:18 57
  3:19 52

12 20
12:10 58
21:27 67
22:33 67

www.ingramcontent.com/pod-product-compliance
Lightning Source LLC
Chambersburg PA
CBHW071244070526
44583CB00017B/2315